"We Western and overeducated preachers tend to get too conceptual and cerebral in the pulpit. No wonder the people think we have 'nothing' to say. These short and usable stories for all the Sundays in the Lectionary cycle, wonderfully collected by Gerard Fuller, reveal a preaching that is alive, touching, humorous, and demanding. I would like to hear his sermons—and yours after you read this book."

Richard Rohr, O.F.M.
San Antonio Friary
Albuquerque, NM

"One of my students in homiletics asked if I could give him the title of the best collection of stories available for use in preaching. I told him to give me a day to think about it. The next day Gerard Fuller's book arrived in the mail. I had my answer! Fuller's book is a gold mine for preachers in search of stories for all the Sundays of the liturgical cycle.

"I'm recommending this book to all my friends whether they preach or simply enjoy good stories. God's Word is alive and well in *Stories for All Seasons*."

Andre Papineau
Author, *Let Your Light Shine*
and *Lightly Goes the Good News*

"Father Fuller's *Stories for All Seasons* is a treasure chest of narrative gems! It is filled with stories (both delightfully short and rich in meaning) that teach, inspire, amuse, encourage, and provoke. Once I started reading this wonderful book, I had a hard time putting it down. Fuller claims these stories are for every Sunday, every year, every preacher, every teacher. He's right. But I would add, they are for every day and for everyone."

Melannie Svoboda, S.N.D.
Author, *Teaching Is Like . . . Peeling Back Eggshells*
and *Jesus, I'm a Teacher, Too*

GERARD FULLER, O.M.I.

Stories
for All Seasons

for every Sunday

every Year

every Preacher

every Teacher

TWENTY-THIRD PUBLICATIONS
THE COLUMBA PRESS

Third printing 1999

Published simultaneously:

Twenty-Third Publications
185 Willow Street
P.O. Box 180
Mystic, CT 06355
860-536-2611
800-321-0411

ISBN 0-89622-643-3
Library of Congress Catalog Card Number 94-61853

The Columba Press
55A Spruce Avenue
Stillorgan Industrial Park
Blackrock, Co. Dublin, Ireland

ISBN 1-85607-145-6

Printed in the U.S.A.

Acknowledgment

A book of this kind relies on many different sources: books on storytelling and preaching, newsletters and periodicals of stories and anecdotes for preachers, and the like. Those directly cited are listed on pages 135-147, for which the author of this volume acknowledges his gratitude for permission to reprint. In a few instances, the source of a story could not be ascertained.

Contents

Introduction   1

════════ Year A ════════

Advent   6
Christmas Season   9
Lent   13
Easter   18
Ordinary Time   25

════════ Year B ════════

Advent   47
Christmas Season   50
Lent   54
Easter   61
Ordinary Time   69

════════ Year C ════════

Advent   91
Christmas Season   94
Lent   98
Easter   102
Ordinary Time   111

Sources   135

Notes   138

Stories for ALL Seasons

Introduction

The use of stories in speaking of God is age-old. The Old Testament is full of stories: The Garden of Eden, Noah and the Ark, Jonah and the Whale. The Song of Songs is an extended love story.

Jesus, who knew the power of stories, used them to proclaim the kingdom. Who can forget the images and messages of the stories he told? The Prodigal Son, the Good Samaritan, the Sower of Seed, the Publican and Sinner in the Temple. Mark tells us: "With many such parables he spoke the word to them, as they were able to hear it; he did not speak to them without a parable. . ." (4:33). We can't imagine Jesus speaking without stories.

The more readable theologians are the ascetical theologians, because they tell us stories. Read John of the Cross, St. Teresa of Avila, Meister Eckhart, and other mystics. Then there are the professional storytellers who by their craft teach us theology and spirituality: Antoine de Saint-Exupéry, J.D. Salinger, Graham Greene, Flannery O'Connor. Storytelling and theology have been bedfellows since time out of mind.

People are attracted by stories. They appeal to our eyes with their color; our ears with their melody, words, sounds; our minds with their images of harsh military battles or tender love scenes. Begin to tell a story and even the day-dreamer will begin to listen intently.

Stories attract by their suspense, including those in Scripture. Will the Prodigal Son come home again and how will he be received? Will the seed grow? Why did the Samaritan stop to help the injured Jew? Why did the Master pay those who came to work last as much as those who came first?

Our world, for better or worse, is full of stories. They keep us tied to our television sets. We go to movies, musicals, and dramas because we want to be a part of the competition, the conflict, the romance, the suspense—all that makes life interesting.

Recently, John Shea focused our attention on the place of stories in homilies with his own stories and poems. William J. Bausch does the same in his books, *Storytelling: Imagination and Faith* and *Storytelling the Word* (Twenty-Third Publications, 1988 and 1996).

Stories are, in a word, an integral part of human life; one can't be imagined without the other. In fact, to use the words of John and Mary Harrell *(To Tell of Gideon)*, humans are "the creatures who think in stories." Stories give us a jumping-off point. They are the vehicle by which we discover our own story. We hear a story and we go down into our subconscious (unconsciously, of course), where we check out those times and actions in our lives that correspond to the story. We recognize our own story in the stories of others. When this happens, we have an experience of discovery, an illumination that enables us to know ourselves and God better, more than any abstraction or definition can. We discover "truth" in stories more than in any other way. That's why myths, and saga, and epic poems are ancient vehicles of truth.

Stories deal with intuition, our most direct contact with God. They allow us to see God by way of analogy: "God is like. . . ." Without this approach, we can know little if anything about God except through divine inspiration, through the revelation given to us, the church. And even this revelation comes to us through wildly imaginative stories, such as we see in the prophets, in Jesus' parables, and in the Book of Revelation.

Children come to know themselves and the world through stories. I spent my boyhood reading about King Arthur and the Knights of the Round Table. Is not the preacher a knight seeking the "Holy Grail"? One of the most telling influences on my childhood was a book entitled *The Winning Basket*. It taught me much

about life, especially about perseverance. Maybe that's why bas-
ketball was my obsession from age 10 to 35.

Stories in homilies are not to be used for their own sake. In preparing a Sunday homily, I read some 20 homily resources and I
end up with two or three typewritten pages, single-spaced, of stories and illustrations. I hate to discard many of them—they're
really good—but if they do not fit into the theme and work toward a coherent whole, out they go.

For each Sunday of the liturgical year, following the Lectionary
cycle, I present five elements:

•Assigned Gospel citation. It would be wise to read the Gospel
in its entirety before examining the remaining elements.

•Brief scriptural tag, or title, summing up the incident por-
trayed in the Gospel.

•Theme, which gives one of many possible themes a preacher
or teacher can use for that Gospel. I often use the theme taken
from a homily I wrote.

•Story, or anecdote, always comes from a homily I wrote for
that Sunday. It may be taken from a section of the homily that de-
velops a subsidiary idea, and thus is proper to that section and
may not seem to apply to the theme.

•Application, often in the form of a question, is a suggestion
for the preacher, teacher, or layperson hoping to apply the Gospel
in a gospel-centered homily, in classroom instruction, or for spiritual reading.

The classic homily structure has three points. A story used in
the first part would not fit well in the third part, and vice versa.
Each story highlights the point being made in the part of the homily from which it is taken.

Some stories work well in the introduction. An introductory
story is meant to capture attention. However, it should lead into a
statement of the theme of the homily. It often performs both func-
tions well if it is humorous, or interesting for some other reason,
such as timeliness. This initial story should not be so funny or oth-
erwise odd that it distracts from or obscures the theme statement,
or engenders a false attitude or expectation. The preacher is not a
stand-up comedian.

Stories in the middle of the homily should support the theme in that part by means of illustration, example, or exposition. Such stories might be of some length. An entire homily can be built around one long story that is well woven to bring out the theme.

Stories near the sermon's end may serve to build up to a climax, or have an essential or attitudinal effect on the hearer. This is seldom the place for a humorous or light story.

Stories can clarify your message, bring it to life, and touch the hearts of your listeners. I hope you find in these pages stories that speak to you and through you to those you minister to in your preaching.

—— Year A ——

Advent

1st Sunday
Matthew 24:37–44

A Time for Watching
Theme: In Advent we await Jesus, our light.

A teacher introduced a sentence to his students and asked them what they thought of it. The sentence was "Wait for the light." Some thought it was beautiful, others thought it was a good spiritual maxim to live by. Finally, he told them where he read it: on the corner of an intersection that flashed the warning: "Wait for the light."[1]

Application: Do we habitually make important decisions without first praying to Jesus for light?

2nd Sunday
Matthew 3:1–12

John the Baptist Preaches Repentance
Theme: We are to repent and wait for the Lord.

While working on his famous painting, "The Last Supper," Leonardo daVinci had an argument with a certain man. He lashed out against the fellow with bitter words and threatening gestures. When the argument was over, daVinci went back to his canvas where he was working on the face of Jesus. He could not make one stroke. At last he realized what the trouble was. He put down his brush, found the man he had offended, and asked his forgiveness. He returned to his studio and calmly continued painting the face of Jesus.

Application: Who do we need to forgive?

3rd Sunday

Matthew 11:2–11

John the Baptist's Act of Faith in Jesus

Theme: Our faith grows strong under duress.

In her book *Return to Love,* Marianne Williamson points out that a friend said to her, "Marianne, I'm so depressed by world hunger!" Marianne replied: "Do you give five dollars a week to one of the organizations that feed the hungry?" She goes on to say she asks this question because she has noticed how people who participate in solving problems don't seem to be as depressed as those standing on the sidelines doing nothing.[2]

Application: Have we recently gone out of our way to help someone?

4th Sunday

Matthew 1:18–24

Jesus—Emmanuel: God with Us

Theme: In Jesus, God comes to pitch his tent among us.

On a *National Geographic* "Explorer" TV program recently, the story of Sir Ernest Henry Shackleton (1873-1922) was told. Shackleton was a British explorer who commanded a south polar expedition in 1907-1909, during which Mt. Erebus on Antarctica was climbed, the south magnetic pole was located, and the plateau was crossed to within 100 miles of the South Pole.

In 1915, Shackleton led . . . an expedition to Antarctica which nearly ended in tragedy. His ship got caught in ice and eventually was crushed. The crew had to flee, taking with them what provisions they could carry. They drifted 180 miles on an ice floe to Elephant Island where there was an old supply hut. From there Shackleton and a few of his men sailed 800 miles in a small boat on wild seas to South Georgia Island. After a near tragic landing (the rudder broke apart just as they reached a rocky shore), they made a nearly impossible crossing of the rugged mountain range to a whaling village on the opposite shore.

Meanwhile, the men he left behind at Elephant Island had exhausted their supplies and had nearly given up hope that the "boss"—that's what they called Shackleton—would make it back to save them. But he did, and one can only imagine the excitement of those beleaguered men the day they sighted Shackleton's rescue ship making its way through the stormy Antarctic Ocean to Elephant Island. The "boss" had arrived, just as he said he would.[3]

Application: Are we faithfully living in expectation of our Lord's coming?

The Birth of the Lord
Luke 2:1–14

Jesus Is Born
Theme: Jesus "pitches his tent" among us.

The custom of placing lighted candles in the windows at Christmas was brought to America by the Irish. When religion was suppressed throughout Ireland during the English persecution, the people had no churches. Priests hid in forests and caves and secretly visited the farms and homes to say Mass there during the night. It was the dearest wish of every Irish family that at least once in their lifetimes a priest would arrive at Christmas to celebrate Mass on this holiest of nights. For this grace they hoped and prayed all through the year.

When Christmas came, they left their doors unlocked and placed burning candles in the windows so that any priest who happened to be in the vicinity could be welcomed and guided to their home through the dark night. Silently the priest would enter through the unlatched door and be received by the devout inhabitants with fervent prayers of gratitude and tears of happiness that their home was to become a church for Christmas.

To justify this practice in the eyes of the English soldiers, the Irish people explained that they burned the candles and kept the doors unlocked so that Mary and Joseph, looking for a place to stay, would find their way to their home and be welcomed with open hearts. The English authorities, finding this Irish "superstition" harmless, did not bother to suppress it. The candles in the windows have always remained a cherished practice of the Irish, although many of them have long since forgotten the earlier meaning.[4]

Application: What makes Christmas "real" for us?

The Holy Family

Matthew 2:13–15, 19–23

Flight Into Egypt

*Theme: Families must turn to the Holy Family
in their desert experiences.*

One family gathered to celebrate the holiday without much thought to its significance. Little Charlotte, gulping her milk, heaved a white-mustached sigh. Then she pointed her fork toward her grandfather like a microphone and asked, "Grandpa, why is today called Christmas?" The child's question came like a peal of thunder. "Out of the blue it fell crashing into the dining room just as though, indeed, the roof might be collapsing." Did the little girl have any idea what she was asking? After what seemed like an eternity her grandfather said, "Perhaps your mother could give you a better answer than I could." It had been a trying day for Rita, her mother. It was the first time she was able to sit with her father in many years. She answered her daughter: "Today is called Christmas, Charlotte, because it is the birthday of Jesus Christ." She then gave a brief explanation. Grandpa looked in disbelief at his daughter. . . .She spoke almost as though she had just discovered the origins of Christmas herself, as if that very moment such knowledge had been revealed to her.[5]

Application: To make Christmas come alive, it would be good for each family member, gathered around the table, to express what Christmas means to him or her.

Solemnity of Mary

Luke 2:16–21

Mary treasured these events in her heart.

Theme: For Mary, family came first.

In his new book, *All Rivers Run to the Sea* (Knopf, 1995), Elie Wiesel recalls the terrible moment when his family had to make a critical choice. The war was coming to an end, but the deportation of Jews continued. Elie (who was 15 at the time), his parents, and three sisters faced deportation from their village in Hungary to the concentration camp at Birkenau. Maria, a Christian and the family's housekeeper, begged the Wiesels to hide in her family's cabin in the mountains. At first, the Wiesels declined, but Maria persisted. The family gathered at the kitchen table for a family meeting: should they go with Maria, or stay and take their chances?

The family decided to stay. Elie Wiesel remembers:

"But why?" [Maria] implored us, her voice breaking.

"Because," my father replied, "a Jew must never be separated from his community. What happens to everyone else happens to us as well." My mother wondered aloud whether it might not be better "to send the children with Maria." We protested: We're young and strong. The trip won't be as dangerous for us. If anyone should go with Maria, it's you. After a brief discussion, we thanked Maria. "My father was right. We wanted to stay together, like everyone else. Family unity is one of our most important traditions…the strength of the family tie, which had contributed to the survival of our people for centuries…"

The war did not end soon enough for the Wiesels. Only Elie and two of his sisters survived. His mother, father, and youngest sister died in the camps.[6]

Application: Mary treasured family. The suffering and the joy. Do we rate family as one of our highest values? In what practical ways do we show it?

Epiphany
Matthew 2:1–12

The Magi
Theme: The world comes to Jesus for wisdom.

That great philosopher of the comic strips, Charlie Brown, thought he knew his way through life. Lucy says to him, "Life is a mystery, Charlie Brown. Do you know the answer?" Charlie Brown answers, "Be kind. Don't smoke. Be prompt. Smile a lot.

Eat sensibly. Avoid cavities, and mark your ballot carefully. Avoid too much sun . . ." As Charlie drones on, Lucy walks away.[7]

Application: Are we truly willing to risk something important to us to find Jesus?

Baptism of the Lord
Matthew 3:13–17

John Baptizes Jesus
Theme: Jesus receives his calling from the Father.

One of the most dramatic moments in the program "Roots" by Alex Haley is the "eight day" ceremony when Omorro gives his newborn son, Kunta Kinte, his name and the child becomes a member of the tribe. In the culture of western Africa, the name given a child is both a gift and a challenge. Haley describes the naming rite:

"[Omorro] lifted the infant, and as all watched, whispered three times into his son's ear the name he had chosen for him. It was the first time the name had ever been spoken as the child's name, for Omorro's people felt that each human being should be the first to know who he was."

That night the father completed the ceremony: "Out under the moon and the stars, alone with his son that eighth night, Omorro completed the naming ritual. Carrying little Kunta in his strong arms, he walked to the edge of the village, lifted his baby up with his face to the heavens and said, softly, 'Behold the only thing greater than yourself.'"[8]

Application: Jesus is even greater than all creation, and baptism makes us one with Jesus.

Lent

1st Sunday

Matthew 4:1–11

Temptation in the Desert

Theme: Scripture must be our refuge,
a source of light, in time of temptation.

Why do we need this time [of Lent]? For one thing, we need to reflect on how easily we slip from slight sins to bigger sins. For example, the newspapers recently carried a story about an Alabama man who planned to profit from a simple burglary. He entered a house and began clearing out the valuables. He came across a .44 Magnum and accidentally shot himself in the calf with it. However, despite the fact that a .44 Magnum makes a very painful, dangerous wound, he obviously could not take his problem to the hospital. About this time, the woman who lives at the house returned home.

So the burglar felt he had no choice but to tie her up. That added seriously to his original burglary offense. Now wounded, the man needed a car. He stole the woman's. Grand theft—auto. However, pain and loss of blood from his leg wound were causing him to drive rather erratically. That attracted the attention of a police officer.

The burglar pulled off the road in his car and the policeman pulled up behind him. The fleeing criminal, now desperate, shot through the windshield of the patrol car and wounded the officer. However, the patrol car was still moving forward and managed to run over the shooter. Although the car didn't do much damage because the burglar was in a ditch as the car passed over him, neither that nor the complication of the attempted murder of a police officer was improving his day.

Next, the Alabama man fled into the woods on foot. Somewhere back in the woods, he apparently came close to a moonshine still or a marijuana patch. At least that is the best explanation for why someone put three .22 caliber slugs in his posterior.

Now, obviously in no shape to walk, he stole another vehicle. However, he actually had to crawl to this car. When police finally captured the man, he had been shot four times and run over once. He faces charges for attempted murder, armed robbery, assault with a deadly weapon, two counts of grand theft-auto, and a host of lesser crimes.[9]

Application: Do we think that living by Scripture is only for Evangelicals and Fundamentalists?

2nd Sunday

Matthew 17:1–9

The Transfiguration

Theme: Jesus gives us a vision to live by: himself.

Rabbi Abraham Twersky tells a story about his great-grandfather who was sitting with other rabbinical scholars studying the Talmud when it was decided to take a break for refreshments. One of the group offered to pay for the refreshments, but there was no one who volunteered to go for them. According to Twersky, in his book *Generation to Generation,* his great-grandfather said, "Just hand me the money, I have a young boy who will be glad to go."

After a rather extended period, he finally returned with the refreshments, and it became obvious to all that the rabbi himself had gone and performed the errand. Noticing their discomfort, the rabbi explained: "I didn't mislead you at all. You see, many people outgrow their youth and become old men. I have never let the spirit of my youth depart. And as I grew older, I always took along with me that young boy I had been. It was that young boy in me that did the errand."[10]

Application: Our transformation begins in our change of attitude.

3rd Sunday

John 4:5–42

The Woman at the Well
Theme: Jesus provides us with living water.

Some time ago, Hurricane Andrew devastated southern Florida. Houses were leveled, trees were uprooted, human lives were severely disturbed. To cope with this chaos, the National Guard was called out to restore a semblance of order and to respond to immediate human needs. One of the first things the Guard did in the midst of people whose lives had been devastated by water and wind was to supply clean drinking water. In the midst of so much loss, clean drinking water was absolutely necessary to sustain health and life. You may recall the image of a National Guardsman standing next to a tanker truck dispensing clean drinking water to those who were victimized by Hurricane Andrew.

More recently we saw the same scene in Rwanda, where thousands died of cholera until the UN could get America and other nations to set up clean water systems to supply life-giving water to the dying.

Application: Do we go to Jesus, who alone can satisfy our thirst, as our fountain of water springing up to eternal life?

4th Sunday

John 9:1–41

The Blind Man
Theme: Jesus is the light of the world.

A man told about a trip he took with his little boy, two and a half years old. It was the first time the father and the boy had been away by themselves—just the two of them. The first night they spent in a hotel, the father moved his bed close to the little boy's, and when they were both tucked in, he turned out the light. After after a few minutes, a little voice said: "It sure is dark, isn't it?"

"Yes," said the father, "it's pretty dark, but everything is all right." There was silence for a few more minutes, and then a little hand reached over and took the father's hand. "I'll just hold your hand," said the little boy, "in case you get scared."[11]

Application: What decisions have we recently made because Jesus is our light?

5th Sunday

John 11:1–45

Jesus Raises Lazarus

Theme: Jesus came to give us the ultimate healing: eternal life.

A fellow walked into a doctor's office and the receptionist asked him what he had. He said, "Shingles." So she took down his name, address, medical insurance number and told him to have a seat. Fifteen minutes later a nurse's aide came out and asked him what he had. He said, "Shingles."

So she took down his height, weight, a complete medical history, and told him to wait in the examining room. A half-hour later a nurse came in and asked him what he had. He said, "Shingles." So she gave him a blood test, a blood pressure test, an electrocardiogram, told him to take off all his clothes, and wait for the doctor.

An hour later the doctor came in and asked him what he had. He said, "Shingles." The doctor said, "Where?" He said, "Outside in the truck. Where do you want 'em?"[12]

Application: In what way does our belief in Jesus help us deal with death, even our own death? Or does it?

Passion (Palm) Sunday

Matthew 27:11–54

The Passion

Theme: By his passion and death Jesus redeems us.

After years of wandering, Clint Dennis realized something important was missing from his life. He decided to attend church. As he entered a church for the first time he noticed people putting on long robes. They were also tying ropes around their waists and wrapping headdresses around their heads. "Come, be a part of the mob," a stranger told him.

It was Palm Sunday and the church was re-enacting the Crucifixion in costume. He would be part of the crowd that shouted, "Crucify him! Crucify him!" Hesitantly he agreed. Then another stranger hurried up to him. "The man who is supposed to play one of the thieves on the cross didn't show up," he said. "Would you take his place?" Again Clint agreed and was shown to the cross where he would look on as Jesus died.

Just then, though, something about Clint's manner caught a member's eye. He turned to Clint and asked, "Have you ever asked Jesus to forgive your sins?" "No," Clint replied softly, "but that's why I came here." There beneath the cross, they prayed, and Clint asked Jesus to come into his heart. What the church didn't know was that Clint had been in prison for ten years. He was a real thief. Even after his release he had gone on stealing cars and trucks until he realized that something was missing from his life.[13]

Application: Have we drawn on Jesus' passion and death as a source of strength to forgive others—and ourselves?

Easter

Easter Sunday

John 20:1–9

The Resurrection

Theme: As Jesus has risen, so we who believe in him shall rise with him.

For centuries the butterfly has been a symbol of Easter; the stubby little caterpillar reborn in the cocoon as a majestic butterfly is nature's parable of the Easter mystery. The Greek language uses one and the same word for butterfly and the human soul: Psyche. In Greek mythology, the god of the flesh, Eros, was pictured in amorous pursuit of the butterfly, Psyche. The early Church at Rome adapted the fable in the sacred decorations of the catacombs. The butterfly Psyche became the symbol of the soul . . . lifted above the earthly plane by the great love of God.[14]

Application: Are we living the new life of one risen in Christ that we are called to? How?

2nd Sunday

John 20:19–31

Doubting Thomas

Theme: Jesus calls us to live by faith, not by sight.

A Chinese peasant had a horse. One day the horse ran away. His neighbor came and said, "That's a shame that you lost that horse. It was so valuable." The farmer said,"Well, who knows? How can you tell?"

The next day the horse came back, and brought back with it a dozen wild horses. The neighbor came over and said, "How wonderful that your horse could escape, and then come back and bring a dozen wild horses with it. Now you are indeed a rich man. That's a gift of God." The farmer said, "Well, how do you know? Who can tell?"

The next day, the farmer's son broke his leg riding one of the wild horses. The neighbor came over and said, "That's a terrible thing to have happen. That's awful." The farmer said, "Well, I don't know. Who knows? How can you tell?"

The next day, the army procurement department came by to pick up the son to join the army. He wasn't able to go because he had a broken leg. The neighbor said, "My, that's wonderful, isn't it?" The farmer said, "I don't know. How can you tell?"[15]

Application: Only when we are willing to go beyond appearances will we come to know the assurance, faith, and joy of living in the risen Lord.

3rd Sunday
Luke 24:13–35

On the Road to Emmaus
Theme: We see Jesus alive in his word,
in the breaking of bread, and in the community of believers.

Archbishop Rembert Weakland of Milwaukee said in an interview in the magazine *The Critic:* "If younger people are having an identity problem as Catholics, I tell them to do two things: Go to Mass every Sunday, and work in a soup kitchen. If one does those two things over a period of time, then something will happen to give one a truly Catholic identity. The altar and the marketplace— these two—must be related to each other; when they are, one works better, and one prays better."[16]

Application: Is our celebration of the Eucharist completed by our loving deeds?

4th Sunday

John 10:1–10

The Good Shepherd
Theme: Jesus shepherds us with loving vigilance.

In her book *Lessons of the Heart* (Ave Maria Press), Pat Livingston describes an afternoon when Claire, her niece, introduced her stuffed animals and dolls to Pat, calling them by name and describing when they were born. The four-year-old told Pat all about what these friends had done, the times they had been good, the times Claire had had to spank them. She pointed out the ones who never went to bed on time. The next day after Pat returned home she received a phone call from her sister. Claire had drawn four stick figures—one of whom had a head with small circles on each side. The figures were Claire's mother, father, older brother, and Aunt Pat. "What are those things on Aunt Pat's head?" asked Claire's mother. "They're ears," her daughter responded. "Aunt Pat really listens. That makes me feel special."[17]

Application: Do we believe that Jesus listens to us? Do we take our cares to him, the Good Shepherd?

5th Sunday

John 14:1–12

Jesus Prepares a Place for Us
Theme: Jesus and the Father are one.

A beggar came every week to beseech a wealthy philanthropist for charity. Every week the rich man listened to his tale of woe and graciously doled out a generous gift. One day, the philanthropist took the beggar aside and said to him, "Listen, you know I will continue giving you a nice amount every week. You don't have to convince me any more. A little less cringing, a little less whining about your condition, and we would both be happier." The beggar drew himself up to the full stature of his ragged pride and dignity. "My good sir," he replied indignantly, "I don't teach you how to be a millionaire; please don't teach me how to be a beggar."[18]

Application: Jesus teaches us how to go to the Father. It's up to us to follow the route. Or do we choose to do it "my way"?

6th Sunday
John 14:15–21

Jesus Promises the Holy Spirit
Theme: We now walk in the Spirit Jesus promised us.

Dorothy Pryse was listening to a Christian radio station as she drove to the grocery store one morning. A person was talking about kindness. Then he said, "I wonder how many of you are listening to me on your car radio and thinking of how you can be kind while driving?" Dorothy began thinking about what he was saying. A few blocks away, she saw a woman waiting in her car to come out of her driveway. Traffic was heavy; Dorothy knew this woman would have a hard time getting out. She slowed down to let her out. The woman smiled and waved at her.

When she got to the grocery store she saw a parking space. As she started pulling in, another car on the opposite side also started pulling in. Dorothy backed out and found another parking spot. As they both got out of their cars, the driver of the other car said, "I can't believe what you just did. Anyone else would have made me back out."

Dorothy explained what she had heard on the radio about showing love. The two women began talking. Dorothy discovered the woman had just moved into the area, didn't know anyone, and was looking for a church. "I invited her to come to our church," Dorothy says, "and a strong friendship has blossomed from our chance meeting and a small act of kindness."[19]

Application: Does our Spirit-life blossom in acts of kindness? How?

7th Sunday

John 17:1–11

Jesus Prays for the Apostles

Theme: Prayer must be an integral part of our life as it was for Jesus.

Dr. Harry Ironside used to tell a story about a group of dissidents who left a church to begin what they hoped would be the "perfect church." The new congregation considered themselves to be such a spiritual blessing to God that they put a sign outside their church: "JESUS ONLY!" The church didn't reach out to their community, however; they only ministered to themselves. One day when Dr. Ironside went by the church, he noticed that the first three letters had fallen off their sign to reveal a new message: "US ONLY!" The new message revealed the truth about that church's ministry.[20]

Application: Do we pray for unity—among religions, in the neighborhood, among nations?

Pentecost

John 20:19–23

The Holy Spirit Comes Upon the Church

Theme: The Holy Spirit touches all believers.

Alexander the Great once came upon Diogenes, the philosopher, looking intently at a heap of human bones. Alexander asked him, "What are you looking for?" Diogenes answered: "Something I cannot find." "And what is that?" asked Alexander. The philosopher replied, "The difference between your father's bones and those of his slaves."[21]

Application: How might we describe the impact the Spirit has had on our life?

Trinity Sunday

John 3:16–18

"God So Loved . . ."

*Theme: "There remain these three: faith, hope, and love.
But the greatest of these is love" (1 Corinthians 13:13).*

A little girl in an orphanage was a real problem child or so thought the headmistress. One day the mistress saw this child walk outside the main gate—forbidden by the rules of the house. The girl walked to a tree down the block and tied some pieces of paper to a tree. "Aha," thought the headmistress, now I've got her." She went out and retrieved the pieces of paper. On them the little girl had written, "To whoever finds this, I love you."[22]

Application: Loving relationships form the essence of the Trinity. Does it "in-form" our family and community relationships? How?

Corpus Christi

John 6:51–58

The Bread of Life

Theme: Jesus has given himself to us as living bread.

A group of churches and social service organizations have formed the Boston Food Bank. The bank collects thousands of tons of food every year, donated by several large food producers in New England. The bank then distributes the food to the poor and homeless in the Boston area.

But the food bank has had a particular problem making connections with one company, the largest processor of fish sticks in the country. The director of the food bank explains: "We estimate they throw away over a million pounds of fish each year that could be turned back to the community." While local executives seem to support the idea of donating the unused food, "the problem is with the accounting department."

That's right, says the accounting department. The company says it would cost $400,000 to process the leftovers into plain fish cakes. And because it doesn't now make fish cakes, it can't estimate the fair market value of the giveaways for tax deduction purposes. So, until the accounting department can figure it all out, the company will continue to throw the leftover fish away.[23]

Application: Do we let laws and the bottom line get in the way of helping others?

Ordinary Time

2nd Sunday

John 1:29–34

John the Baptist Recognizes Jesus

Theme: We are to be humble as John the Baptist was before Jesus.

A university student who was having a hard time getting his act together decided to take his frustrations out on God. He went into the university chapel, sat in a pew, looked heavenward and said, "All we have on this earth are problems and a bunch of dummies who will never figure out how to solve them. Even I could make a better world than this one." And somewhere deep inside him the student heard God's answer: "That's what you're supposed to do."[24]

Application: How are we God's hands, arms, and legs—now?

3rd Sunday

Matthew 4:12–23

Jesus Calls John and James

Theme: Jesus calls us as he did his apostles.

A boy in a Sunday School class became increasingly uncomfortable as the teacher spoke about dying and going to heaven. The teacher said, "Put up your hand if you want to go to heaven." Everyone but the one boy put up their hands. The teacher was shocked. "Don't you want to go to heaven?" The boy responded, "Yes, but not with this bunch."[25]

Application: Who are the people we would rather not have to deal with?

4th Sunday
Matthew 5:1–12

The Beatitudes
*Theme: Jesus has blessed the simple way of life
most people live if lived in faith.*

Another who was inspired by the Sermon on the Mount was Dr. Tom Dooley. After graduating from medical school, Dooley enlisted in the Navy as a doctor. The big day of his life came one hot July afternoon off the coast of Vietnam. That's when his ship rescued 1000 refugees who were drifting helplessly in an open boat. Many of the refugees were diseased and sick. Since Dooley was the only doctor on the ship, he had to tackle, single-handedly, the job of giving medical aid to these people. It was backbreaking, but he discovered what a little medicine could do for sick people like this. He said: "Hours later, I stopped a moment to straighten my shoulders and made another discovery—the biggest of my life. I was happy [treating these people] . . . happier than I had ever been before." Dooley's experience that hot July afternoon changed his life forever.[26]

Application: Do we find our fulfillment in works of mercy?

5th Sunday
Matthew 5:13–16

Apostles as Salt and Light
Theme: Disciples of Jesus are meant to change the world.

A young Boy Scout was on maneuvres with his fellow Scouts. They were being trained in first aid methods and how to come to the help of those in need. This Scout's job was to lie on the ground with a red bandage on him and wait for his fellow Scouts to come and administer first aid. He waited, and waited, and waited. When the other troop members did come, they found a note that said, "I have bled to death and gone home."

Application: Concretely, how are we coming to the aid of others?

6th Sunday

Matthew 5:17–37

Sermon on the Mount

Theme: A heart of love is the main factor in our actions.

Several years ago William F. Merton of Mt. Clemens, Michigan, wrote to *Reader's Digest* to tell about a memorable argument he had with his wife. The argument was well under way as they left a party one evening. Once they were in the car, words were flying. The area they were driving through was not the best, so they stopped arguing just long enough to lock the doors. Then they started again. Merton's wife had really worked up a storm, and after a few choice words from him, she shouted, "Stop the car and let me out!" Merton pulled over to the curb. His wife unlocked the door and got out, but then looked around and got back in again. Looking a little sheepish she said, "Take me to a better neighborhood."[27]

Application: How seriously do we take Jesus' warning that our thoughts can be as important as, or more important than, our deeds?

7th Sunday

Matthew 5:38–48

Pray for Your Enemy

Theme: Prayer, not enmity, for our enemy.

Traveling during his term as Vice President, Thomas Jefferson requested a room at Baltimore's principal hotel. The Vice President was traveling alone, without secretary or servants; it had been a long trip and it showed in his clothes and appearance. The proprietor, not recognizing his distinguished guest, refused him a room. After Mr. Jefferson left, the proprietor learned that he had just turned away from his establishment the Vice President of the United States. The horrified proprietor immediately sent his servants out to find Mr. Jefferson and offer him whatever accommodations he wished. A servant found the Vice President at a small inn where he had taken a room for the night. Mr. Jefferson sent the servant back to the hotel's proprietor with this message: "Tell your master I value his good intentions highly, but if he has no room for a dirty farmer, he shall have none for this Vice President."[28]

Application: Jesus is in the least and shabbiest-looking person, especially if we consider that person our enemy.

8th Sunday
Matthew 6:24–34

No One Can Serve Two Masters
Theme: Purity of heart: Seek God alone.

Benjamin Reaves tells about a little fellow whose mother had died. His father was trying hard to be both Mom and Dad under difficult circumstances. The father had scheduled a picnic for the two of them. The little fellow had never been on a picnic. He was excited—so excited that he couldn't sleep. Soon there was the patter of little feet down the hall to where his father was sleeping. He shook his Dad who would have responded gruffly except he saw the expression on his little son's face. "What's the matter, son?" he asked. The fellow said, "Oh, Daddy, tomorrow's going to be so wonderful. I just can't sleep I'm so excited."

The father laughed and said, "Son, it won't be wonderful if we don't get some sleep. Now you go back to your bedroom and try to sleep."

A while later the ritual was repeated. The father was already sleeping soundly, when the boy placed an excited hand on his shoulder. "What do you want now?" his father asked.

"Daddy," said the boy, "I just want to thank you for tomorrow."[29]

Application: Do we trust our Father in heaven to take care of us "for tomorrow?" Do we thank God in advance for doing so?

9th Sunday

Matthew 7:21–27

End of Sermon on the Mount
Theme: Following God's law is prudence.

Someone said even the devil can quote scripture for his own ends. Have we ever been like the terrible-tempered Lucy in the "Peanuts" comic strip? Lucy comes into the room where Linus is watching TV. He says to her, "I was here first, so I get to watch what I want." Without a word Lucy marches to the set and flips the channel to her program. Linus protests. "Hey!" Assuming her best know-it-all stance, Lucy intones, "In the 19th chapter of the book of Matthew it says, 'Many that are first will be last, and the last first.'" Linus's response to this paradox sounds like something you or I would say. He mutters, "I'll bet Matthew didn't have an older sister."[30]

Application: Do we ever quote scripture more for show than for truth?

10th Sunday

Matthew 9:9–13

Jesus Calls Matthew
Theme: Perseverance is needed in following Jesus.

We Americans are suckers for the underdog. We ought to appreciate the story of Samuel Logan Brengle. Brengle gave up an opportunity to pastor one of the largest churches in Mid-America in order to join the ranks of the Salvation Army when that organization was just getting established in the United States. One of his early assignments was in Danbury, Connecticut, where Brengle's entire congregation often numbered less than a dozen people.

Determined to reach Danbury with the Gospel, each evening Brengle marched up and down its streets singing, preaching, and praising God.

One night, while marching with only two of his parishioners at his side, a large lame black man and a little hunchback girl, Brengle and his "congregation" were bravely singing a song, ironically entitled, "We're the Army That Shall Conquer." Suddenly, the small group came abreast a large and imposing Methodist Church. As Brengle surveyed that impressive edifice a voice seemed to say to him, "You fool, you! You might have been the pastor of a great church like that. But here you are instead, the pastor of a lame man and a little hunchback!" For a moment his voice faltered and his resolve weakened. But only for a moment. His thoughts turned to the many ways God had been dealing with him, and with a new sense of determination, he swung his arm vigorously and began leading his tiny band once again in singing "We're the Army That Shall Conquer!"[31]

Application: Do we think St. Matthew at times wondered if he should have remained a tax collector? What do we do in times of doubt about serious decisions we have made? How determined are we to carry on to the best of our insights and abilities?

11th Sunday

Matthew 9:36—10:8

Jesus Chooses Twelve Apostles
Theme: As apostles, we must have compassion on the crowds.

A bishop in the South of London came out of his cathedral one day and saw a small boy playing in the gutter. He asked him what he was doing with the mud. "I'm making a cathedral," he said. "Well," said the bishop, "if you have a cathedral, you must have a bishop." "Nah," said the boy, "I ain't got enough muck to make a bishop."[32]

Application: How do we see authority? Would we agree with the boy, or are the bishops getting a bad rap? Why?

12th Sunday

Matthew 10:26–33

"Every Hair of Your Head . . ."
Theme: The Father's providence answers all our cares.

Jim Moore recalls being five and at his grandmother's house when a fierce storm broke out. His father had to come get him. The wind was blowing; rain was pelting down; lightning was flashing; thunder was rumbling behind the clouds. The storm showed no signs of letting up. . . .Jim's father was wearing a big blue weather coat, and said, "Son, come here." He covered his young son with his coat, and out into the storm they went. Even though it was raining hard, the wind was howling, and he couldn't see a thing under that coat, young Jim was not at all afraid. He knew his father could see where they were going, so he just held on tightly and trusted him. Soon the coat opened and they were home.[33]

Application: In what recent acts have we truly trusted in the Father alone?

13th Sunday

Matthew 10:37–42

Jesus Must Be Our Life
Theme: Baptism calls us to help others,
even to suffer and give our life, for Jesus' sake.

Hospitality is a form of dying to ourselves to serve others. People who can teach us how to die to ourselves to serve, are our friends, like the farmer who was putting up a fence with another young farmer, to help a neighboring farmer. The first farmer suddenly dropped a heavy fence post right in the middle of a mud puddle. Both men were splashed with mud. Later, an eyewitness asked the first farmer, "Jim, did you drop that post in the puddle on purpose?" The farmer nodded his head, saying, "Yes, I sure did." Puzzled, the man asked him why he would do a thing like that.

The farmer grinned and said, "Why, Willy, the boy I was working with had on a new pair of overalls. And we weren't getting any work done because he was so worried about getting dirty. So I dropped the post in the mud hole and got him dirty. Did you notice how much faster the work went after the baptism?"[34]

Application: How ready are we to put all things aside that get in the way of following Jesus?

14th Sunday
Matthew 11:25–30

"Come to Me"
Theme: Jesus is our support.

In Sierra Leone, West Africa, a preacher, David Wiggington, says people learn how to carry heavy burdens on their heads. "He said he learned of a woman in the capital city whose regular employment was that of being a 'human delivery truck.' Her assignment in this capital city of Freetown was to deliver engine blocks from one repair shop to other repair shops. Four men would lift the engine block onto a tray that she carried on her head and off she would go across town carrying this enormous weight. One day this lady came to her destination and found that no one was there to assist her in taking the load off her head. She waited as long as you can wait with an engine block on your head and decided to try to remove it herself. In so doing, she broke her neck and died."[35]

Application: Jesus has commissioned us to help support others in their burdens. How are we doing this?

15th Sunday
Matthew 13:1–23

Parable of the Seed
Theme: We are to bear fruit, leaving to God the measure.

Temple University in Philadelphia came into being through the seed money of a little girl in that city who wanted to attend Sunday school but couldn't because the classes were full. The church was so small that there seemed no place for her. She began saving pennies to build a larger church. Death removed the little girl, but under her pillow was found an old, red pocketbook in which were 57 pennies and a scrap of paper on which was written the reason why she was saving her pennies. The pastor who conducted the funeral told the story of those 57 pennies and it got into the newspapers. What could a little girl's 57 pennies do? Well, they did much. The tide of gifts which her example inspired flowed with increasing strength, and in six years the 57 pennies had become $250,000 which became the nucleus of yet grander things, for the Baptist Temple, with its Good Samaritan Hospital, and the great Temple University, which with its thousands of students, have come into being as the marvelous harvest of a little girl's seed pennies.[36]

Application: How do we support the many good ministries in our parish?

16th Sunday

Matthew 13:24–43

Wheat Among the Weeds
Theme: God allows creation to work itself out.

One day, when the inimitable Groucho Marx was getting off an elevator, he met a priest who immediately recognized the famous comedian. The excited clergyman extended his hand, saying, "I want to thank you for all the joy you've put into the world." Groucho replied, "And I want to thank you, Father, for all the joy you've taken out of it."[37]

Application: Many of us become so concerned with pulling out the weeds we lose the sense of hope and spirit of joy. Do we experience deep joy because we are disciples of Jesus?

17th Sunday

Matthew 13:44–52

Hidden Treasures

Theme: The Kingdom of God is a treasure found in daily life.

Ron DelBene was searching for answers in his life. Someone told him about a man in Los Angeles who has a reputation for being a very wise spiritual guide. On a business trip to the west coast Ron made an appointment to see this wise man. . . .All he could think about was the upcoming meeting with the one who surely had the Answer.

He drove up the coast only to discover on arrival that the man was not there. The longer he waited the angrier he became. Finally the man arrived: "I don't know which was greater, my anger or my disappointment," Ron remembers. "This short, slightly built person didn't look at all like the wise man I had pictured. He didn't even have a beard!" ...Ron thought perhaps the teacher would place his hands on my head or heart and I will explode in ecstasy. But Ron didn't. The wise teacher simply rattled off three things Ron should do. Before Ron had a chance to respond or ask any questions the Wise One left the room. Ron felt disappointed and disillusioned. He had traveled all that way and for what?

After Ron returned home, his wife, Eleanor, asked him about his meeting with the guru. She listened intensely to her husband's every word. "He told me that there are three things I must do," Ron said. "One, pray unceasingly. Two, go home and love my wife and children. Three, do what needs to be done." Eleanor looked straight at Ron and said, "Thank God, someone finally told you that!" What the teacher told was true. "In retrospect," Ron writes, the teacher "was a far wiser man than I appreciated at the time."[38]

Application: Our greatest treasure is at home: our family. Do our daily acts reflect this?

18th Sunday

Matthew 14:13–21

Multiplying Loaves and Fishes
Theme: God is concerned about our daily physical needs.

An elderly woman lived in one half of a duplex apartment. She was extremely poor, but a good woman. She prayed a great deal. In the other half of the duplex lived the owner, a man of no faith, no prayer, no religion. He often made fun of the old lady's trust in God. One day this woman was praying, quite loudly, telling the Lord that she had no food in the house. The godless one heard her and decided: "I'm going to play a trick on the old gal." He took a loaf of bread, laid it at her front door, rang the bell, and then hurried back to his apartment, to hear through the wall her cry of delight: "Thank you, Lord, I just knew You wouldn't fail me." With a devilish grin the man came back to her front door and told her: "You silly old woman. You think God answered your prayer. Well, I'm the one who brought that loaf of bread." Undaunted, the old woman exclaimed: "Praise the Lord! He always helps me in my needs, even if He has to use the devil to answer my prayers."[39]

Application: When have we last come to the aid of someone in need?

19th Sunday

Matthew 14:22–33

Peter Walks on the Water
Theme: Our faith tells us that we are to risk all,
relying on God's support.

A man in a mental institution insisted he was Jesus Christ. No therapist had had any luck in disabusing the man of his illusion. Then this therapist visited the man. He asked the man to put his arms out to the side. The therapist measured the man's arms from fingertip to fingertip. He also measured the man from head to foot. The therapist left the room and came back with a hammer and some nails. By now the patient was becoming curious and very uneasy.

"What are you doing?" the patient demanded.

"You are Jesus Christ, aren't you?" asked the therapist.

"Yes, of course," blustered the patient.

"Well, then," said the therapist, putting the pieces of wood into the form of a cross and starting to nail them together, "You should know what I'm doing."

"Wait! Wait!" the patient shouted. "I'm not Jesus Christ! What's the matter, are you crazy or something?"[40]

Application: Anyone who wants to be a disciple of Jesus had better get used to the idea that trust in him may mean that we are willing to "walk on water."

20th Sunday
Matthew 15:21–28

The Syro-Phoenician Woman
Theme: Faith impels us to keep coming back to God,
even when it may seem futile.

A glimmer of hope in the Serbo-Croatian war. A Franciscan Sister of Mercy, herself a Croat who grew up in Serbia, has been working with rape victims from Bosnia as well as trying to find housing for the many refugees. Dressed in her nun's habit, she goes to a door and pleads with those who answer, "I have no place to stay. I'm hungry. Can you take me in?" Croatia is a deeply Catholic country, so the answer to the nun's plea is almost always, "Of course, Sister." Then the nun steps back to let the real refugees with her be seen. They are usually taken in by the family.[41]

Application: How are we to respond when God seems distant and does not answer our prayer?

21st Sunday

Matthew 16:13–20

Peter Confesses Jesus as Messiah
Theme: We must all confess that Jesus is our savior.

There is a story about an irreligious farmer in one of our western states, who gloried in his irreligion, and he wrote a letter to a local newspaper in these words: "Sir: I have been trying an experiment with a field of mine. I plowed it on Sunday. I planted it on Sunday. I cultivated it on Sunday. I harvested it on Sunday. I carted the crop home to the barn on Sunday. And now, Mr. Editor, what is the result? This October I have more bushels to the acre from the field than any of my neighbors have." He expected applause from the editor, who was not known to be a religious man himself. But when he opened the paper the next week, there, sure enough, was his letter printed just as he had sent it, but underneath it was the short but significant sentence: "God does not always settle accounts in October."[42]

Application: Specifically, when did we last show ourselves disciples of Jesus, or witness him in public?

22nd Sunday

Matthew 16:21–27

Jesus Rebukes Peter
Theme: Following Jesus means we must be ready to suffer.

Valerie Price isn't a name you will recognize. According to worldly standards she is a nobody. Last year, though, 23-year-old Valerie Price went to Somalia to work as a nurse. She wanted to help people who had nothing. She wanted to offer them a better way of life. Valerie was concerned about her safety, but nothing would stop her from doing her work. She was in charge of a feeding center in Mogadishu. Through her life-saving efforts, children who had been near starvation were fed. Valerie even established a school so the children could learn and have some hope for the future. Valerie was fortunate to see some of the fruits of her labors. Earlier this year Valerie made the national news. She was killed by armed bandits outside the school she had started. Valerie was willing to risk her life to help other people. Jesus tells us that in losing her life she actually found it.[43]

Application: Are we ready to put ourselves out, endure hardship, or even lose our lives for Jesus?

23rd Sunday

Matthew 18:15–20

Settling Differences

Theme: Dialoguing with one another is a sacrifice we must undertake to build up the community of the faithful, the church.

When a passenger on a Greyhound bus shouted that there was "a bum in the bathroom," he possibly set a new record for misunderstandings. Other passengers relayed the message to the front, where the driver heard "bomb in the bathroom." The bus was evacuated. Interstate 95 southbound was closed, and traffic backed up for 15 miles. Then police and bomb-sniffing dogs searched the bus before the incident was cleared up.[44]

Application: Communication sometimes gets garbled, including in the church. Are we willing to confront others charitably for the sake of principle?

In a recent "Peanuts" comic strip, Lucy is saying to Schroeder, "Do you think I'm the most beautiful girl in the world?" Naturally, she has to ask several times in different ways, until Schroeder, to be rid of her, says, "Yes." Lucy mopes disconsolately, "Even when he says it, he doesn't say it."[45]

Application: If our dialogues do not always go smoothly, have we asked ourselves why? Are we good listeners?

24th Sunday

Matthew 18:21–35

King Forgives Staggering Debt

Theme: We should make every effort to forgive.

You may remember the story of the grandmother celebrating her golden wedding anniversary who told the secret of her long and happy marriage. "On my wedding day, I decided to make a list of ten of my husband's faults which, for the sake of the marriage, I would overlook." A guest asked the woman what some of the faults she had chosen to overlook were. The grandmother replied, "To tell you the truth, I never did get around to making that list. But whenever my husband did something that made me hopping mad, I would say to myself, "Lucky for him that's one of the ten.""[46]

Application: When was the last time it was very difficult to forgive? If we did forgive, how did it feel?

25th Sunday

Matthew 20:1–16

Vineyard Workers Get the Same Wage

Theme: God's ways are not our ways.

A man who needed a job saw an ad in the local paper for a position open at the zoo. He accepted the job and was to dress up as a monkey and perform in one of the cages. All went well for several days and then, as he was going from limb to limb, he fell. "Help, help," he cried. "Shut up," said the lion in the next cage, "or we'll both lose our jobs."[47]

Application: Have we ever risked ridicule because we were loving or just?

26th Sunday

Matthew 21:28–32

One Son Obeys, the Other Doesn't
Theme: Our actions speak louder than our words.

A survey was distributed during a worship service one Sunday morning. Among the questions was, "Do you think there should be an evening Bible Study?" The young pastor was overwhelmed at the response. Over fifty persons indicated that there should be an evening Bible study. The elated pastor began making plans. A day or two later, the wise, experienced lay leader came to visit the pastor. Gently he advised the young man that he had asked the wrong question. Instead of asking, "Do you think there should be a Bible study?" the pastor should have asked, "Are you willing to attend an evening Bible study?" A second questionnaire was issued. This time the question was, "Are you willing to attend Bible study?" The result was quite different from the week before. This time only twelve persons indicated that they would be willing to attend.[48]

Application: Which brother are we?

27th Sunday

Matthew 21:33–43

Vineyard Owner Punishes Unworthy Servants
Theme: Our life is a period of testing for trustworthiness.

Two men from Mars decide to do a little sightseeing on Earth. They realize that to avoid causing a panic they must appear as inconspicuous as possible. They obtain American clothing, learn the language, and in general make themselves as ordinary as possible. During their first day on Earth nobody notices anything unusual about them. At the end of the day they celebrate their successful foray at an exclusive restaurant. As they are paying their check, they are astonished to hear the waiter say, "You guys must be from Mars!"

"What?" asked the dumbfounded Martians. "How can you tell?"

"Well," replied the waiter, "you're the first customers to pay cash since I've been working here."[49]

Application: How can others see from the way we live that we are disciples of Jesus?

28th Sunday
Matthew 22:1–14
Wedding Guest Without a White Robe
Theme: God gives us gratis the robe of grace.

Television journalist Hugh Downs and his wife once attended a function in Washington. When the time came to return to New York, they discovered that their flight had been cancelled due to bad weather. Downs immediately called the front desk and was informed that they could catch a five o'clock train, which was leaving in 45 minutes. Mrs. Downs was showering, and to save time, Hugh hurriedly packed all their belongings, called the bell captain, and asked that the bags be rushed right over to the station and put on the train. A bellhop came immediately and got them. Five minutes later, Mrs. Downs stepped out of the bathroom wrapped in a towel. "Dear," she asked, "would you please hand me my green dress?"[50]

Application: Will we be ready, and wearing the white robe of grace?

29th Sunday
Matthew 22:15–21
"Pay Tribute to Caesar?"
Theme: We are to use the goods of this world to further God's Kingdom.

John Wesley's three-point sermon, in which his first point was "Get all you can." To this, an old rich miser said, "Amen." Next Wesley said, "Keep all you can." Again, the miser said, "Amen."

Then the preacher said, "Give all you can." And the selfish man said, 'What a shame to spoil a good sermon."

On the government side, we have such quips as Arthur Godfrey saying, "I'm proud to be paying taxes in the U.S. The only thing is, I could be just as proud for half the money." Or Will Rogers, who said, "The income tax has made more liars out of the American people than golf has." And Mortimer Caplan, former IRS director, saying, "There is one difference between a tax collector and a taxidermist—the taxidermist leaves the hide."[51]

Application: Do we have our priorities straight about money? Have we ever thought of tithing? If not, why not?

30th Sunday
Matthew 22:34–40

Jesus' Great Commandment
Theme: We must love as Jesus does.

In our nation's archives there is an account of two women from Tennessee who came before President Abraham Lincoln at the conclusion of the Civil War. They were asking for the release of their husbands held as prisoners of war at Johnson's Island. Lincoln put them off until Friday, when they came again. Again the President put them off until Saturday. At each of the interviews one of the ladies stressed to Lincoln that her husband was a religious man.

After the Saturday interview the President ordered the release of the prisoners. Then he turned to this lady and said, "You say your husband is a religious man. Tell him when you meet him, that I say I am not much of a judge of religion. In my opinion, however, the religion that sets men to rebel and fight against their governments . . . [so that they can] eat their bread on the sweat of other men's faces, is not the sort of religion upon which people can get to heaven!"[52]

Application: All the virtues are interconnected. Does our love bear the fruit of justice?

31st Sunday

Matthew 23:1–12

Hypocrisy of the Pharisees
*Theme: Humility in loving action will always
shun the hypocrisy of the Pharisees.*

Love in humble action is had in a story about a monk who was dispatched from one monastery to the other as abbot. When the unknown abbot quietly arrived at his new destination unannounced, the holy monks checked out his humble person and unimpressive demeanor. They immediately sent him to work in their kitchen at the most menial tasks. Uncomplaining, their new abbot spent long hours scouring pots, washing floors, and shelling beans.

Finally, the bishop of the diocese arrived at the monastery. When he could not find the long overdue abbot, he went on a search. Of course, he found him in the kitchen, preparing that night's supper. When he officially presented him to the monks in their chapel, they received a lesson in humility which would last them a lifetime.[53]

Application: Our faith is to be expressed in active love, not empty words. How humble is our love?

32nd Sunday

Matthew 25:1–13

Wise and Foolish Virgins
Theme: Jesus bids us be prepared to meet him.

Our watchfulness must be a daily thing.

"I learned my first lesson in responsibility the day I returned from school to find my guinea pigs missing. I rushed to ask my mother about them.

"'I gave them away because you didn't take care of them.'

"'But I did take care of them!'

"'Joni, I gave them away ten days ago!'"[54]

Application: We can't begin too early to discipline ourselves to be ready for Jesus.

33rd Sunday
Matthew 25:14–30

Servant Who Hid His Talent
Theme: We are to invest our talents while there is still time.

No one can escape the coming of the thief. A burglar broke into a New York firm that manufactures burglar-proof glass by smashing a glass door panel. "It never occurred to us," said the firm's president "to put our own burglar-proof glass in our own door."[55]

Application: What are your dominant talents? Are you using them to benefit others, as befits a disciple of Jesus?

Christ the King
Matthew 25:31–46

Final Judgment
Theme: We will be judged on how we loved our brothers and sisters.

The Parable of the Last Judgment (adaptation):
For I was hungry, and you were obese;
Thirsty and you were watering your lawn;
A stranger and you called the police and were glad to see me taken away;
Naked and you were saying, "I don't have a thing to wear—I must get some new clothes tomorrow";
Ill and you asked,"Is it contagious?"
In prison and you said, "That's where your kind belongs."[56]

The story is told of Martin of Tours who was a Roman soldier and a Christian. One cold winter day, as he was riding into the city, a poor beggar stopped him and asked him for alms. Although Martin had no money, he was moved with compassion for the poor man who stood shivering in the cold. Martin gave him what he had. Taking off his soldier's coat, worn and frayed though it was, he cut it in two and gave half of it to the beggar. That night, Martin had a dream. In his dream he saw heaven and all of the angels and Jesus in the midst of them.

Jesus was wearing half of a Roman soldier's cloak. One of the angels said to him, "Master, why are you wearing that battered old cloak? Who gave it to you?" And Jesus answered softly, "My servant Martin gave it to me."[57]

Application: "What you do to the least of these, you do to me." Does this describe us? Are we glad to know the meaning of these words? Why?

—— Year B ——

Advent

1st Sunday

Mark 13:33–37

Servants Await Owner's Return
Theme: Be alert!

A story comes to us from Eastern mysticism:

A monk asked, "Abbot, what has God's wisdom taught you? Did you become divine?"

"Not at all."

"Did you become a saint?"

"No, as you can clearly see."

"What then, O Abbot?"

"I became awake!"

The abbot might have been reading Mark: "Be on your guard, stay awake. . . ."[1]

Application: What is there in our daily life that shows that we are looking forward to Jesus' coming?

2nd Sunday

Mark 1:1–8

John the Baptist
Theme: Repent!

In the film *The Cemetery Club,* Esther, a middle-aged widow, reflects on the sudden death of her husband, Murray: "By the time the ambulance got there, he was gone. It just seems so unreal, you know? There we were, enjoying a wonderful dinner and. . . When I got home that night, his cigar was still in the ashtray. His toothbrush was still damp. I just couldn't make sense of it, you know? It's like one day you're looking into his face as he proposes and the next day you're standing at his grave remembering how nervous he had been—and, between those two days, 39 years had gone by!"[2]

Application: How are we using our time?

3rd Sunday
John 1:6–8, 19–28

John: A Voice Crying in the Wilderness
Theme: John humbly witnesses Jesus.

An Episcopal priest went into the chancel of the cathedral one Sunday morning and spoke the traditional words: "The Lord be with you," to which the people were to respond: "And with your spirit." Since the nave and the chancel were divided by a distance, the priest was totally dependent on the public address system. The congregation had not heard his opening remarks because two little wires in the microphone were disconnected. Catching the eye of a fellow priest in the chancel, he banged the microphone with his hand. As he did, the two little wires made contact and what he said rather crossly to his fellow priest was broadcast loudly throughout the sanctuary. "There's something wrong with this microphone!" he shouted. And the people gave their patterned response: "And with your spirit."[3]

Application: If the Messiah is present, how do our attitudes, actions, and words reflect the fact of his presence?

4th Sunday
Luke 1:26–38

Annunciation
Theme: Mary opens herself to God's will.

They tell of a man in a small town in South Dakota who tried to give some money back to the Social Security Administration, but could not. At age 65 the man retired from his work as a farm laborer and moved into town. His retirement house was extremely modest, sparsely furnished, and simply kept. Most could not manage on his meager minimum security check.

At the end of the first month of collecting on Social Security, this humble man went to the bank with five dollars in cash and told the teller he wanted to return some money because the government had given him more than he needed. With that request he "blew everybody in the bank away." They explained to him that he couldn't do that, that the government could give out social security funds, but that there was no set-up program for taking any of it back. There was no category for people who wanted to give any of their social security back to the government.[4]

Application: To receive something graciously from another is as much a gift as giving. We can learn from Mary in this regard. When did we last say yes when God asked something difficult of us?

Christmas Season

Birth of the Lord

Luke 2:1–14

Jesus Is Born

Theme: God sends the Son as a baby to a harsh world.

The love of brothers and sisters for one another. That is what Jesus came to give us. The world has commercialized this time of year: it uses the outward trappings of love but has gutted the inner reality.

Tom Wilson shows a cartoon, a carload of people traveling down a snowy highway. The kids are yelling and screaming; the parents are annoyed and short-tempered. Finally they all decide to start singing together. "Over the river and through the woods, To Grandmother's house we go. . . ." In the last frame, you can see the car turning into a driveway. And there, peeking out of a window, are the faces of an elderly couple. Grandmother shakes her head and says to Grandad: "We move over the river and through the woods, and still they find us!"[5]

Application: To speak the truth, Grandmas aren't always sugar and spice, even at Christmas. Let us not sentimentalize giving. How do we cut through the commercialism to get to the real meaning of Christmas?

Holy Family

Luke 2:22–40

Presentation

Theme: The home is a treasure in which we find loving sacrifice.

George was in his seventies. He had never married. Most of his life he was a sailor traveling the oceans of the world. He had no home of his own. His nephew, Bill, always liked Uncle George, so he invited him to live with Bill, his wife, and five children. It was a mutually agreeable arrangement. George now had a home, while Bill's family could travel the world in imagination as they listened to Uncle George recount his experiences.

At times Bill became bored and discontented with family life. How nice it would be to roam the world carefree and footloose. He even expressed this wish. One evening, as Uncle George was telling of some faraway place, he mentioned a map of a buried treasure. The idea stuck in Bill's mind so that when Uncle George died a few years later, Bill went through the old man's few belongings.

Sure enough, there was an envelope addressed to Bill. In it was a map. With shaking fingers and pounding heart he tried to figure out where the treasure was located. Finally he pinpointed the spot. It was his own home, the very spot where he was right now. Uncle George had truly left him a treasure, the realization that his own home, his own family, was a treasure.[6]

Application: How much do we work at making our home a treasure?

Solemnity of Mary

Luke 2:16–21

Mary Treasured These Things in Her Heart
Theme: Mary, Mother, never forgets her children's efforts to pay attention to her.

One Mom had a most revealing experience on her birthday. Her two children ordered her to stay in bed. She lay there looking forward to being brought her breakfast, as the inviting smell of bacon floated up from the kitchen. At last the children called her downstairs. She found them sitting at the table, each with a large plate of bacon and eggs. "As a birthday surprise," one explained, "we've cooked our own breakfast."[7]

Application: A mother's love is inexhaustible. Can we say that about our love for our family, friends, and strangers?

Epiphany of the Lord

Matthew 2:1–12

The Magi

Theme: Three wise men travel far to find the king.

Are we like Gracie Allen, who played the scatterbrained wife in a comedy team with George Burns? Once, Gracie called in a repairman to fix her electric clock. The repairman fiddled with it for a while and then said, "There's nothing wrong with the clock; you didn't have it plugged in." Gracie replied, "I don't want to waste electricity, so I only plug it in when I want to know what time it is."[8]

Application: In what ways do we search for Jesus?

Baptism of the Lord

Mark 1:7–11

Baptism of Jesus

Theme: By our baptism we become sons and daughters of the Father.

There was once a monarch who sought to be the absolute ruler of his domain. He had succeeded in removing all obstacles to his complete control except one: the people still put their ancient god above their king. The king summoned his three wisest advisors to find a way to put an end to such worship. Where, the king asked them, might the people's god be hidden so as to vanish from their lives and cease to threaten the king's rule?

The first advisor suggested hiding the god at the summit of the highest mountain in the kingdom, thousands and thousands of feet high. No, said the king, the people would abandon their homes and climb the mountain to search for it. The second advisor proposed hiding the people's god at the bottom of the sea. The king rejected that idea as well: the people would probe the ocean's depths to find their god again.

The monarch then turned to the third and wisest advisor. The old sage counseled the king, "You should hide the people's god

somewhere in their everyday lives. There they will never find it."
And that is exactly what was done.[9]

*Application: Emmanuel means "God with us." Do we really believe this
and show it in our daily life?*

1st Sunday

Mark 1:12–15

The Temptation of Jesus

Theme: Jesus did not dally with temptation, but turned to God's word. How do we react to temptation?

Is there any purpose to pain? Any advantage to adversity? Any solace in suffering? "Don't be discouraged, Charlie Brown," Schroeder says. "These early defeats help to build character for later on in life."

"For what later on in life?" asks Charlie Brown.

"For more defeats!" replies Schroeder.

Charlie Brown then invests in five cents worth of Lucy's psychiatric help. At first, her advice sounds a bit more sophisticated: "Adversity builds character," she says. "Without adversity a person could never mature and face up to all the things in life!"

"What things?" he asks.

"More adversity!" she says.[10]

Application: Adversity, and a little humor, will see us through Lent and life.

2nd Sunday

Mark 9:2–10

Transfiguration

Theme: Daily life with its temptations follows mountaintop experiences.

A little boy around the turn of the century lived far out in the country. He had reached the age of 12 and had never in all his life seen a circus. Therefore, you can imagine his excitement one day when a poster went up at school that on the next Saturday a traveling circus was coming to town.

He ran home with the glad news, and then came the question: "Dad, can I go?" The family was poor, but the father sensed how important this was to the boy, so he said, "If you will do your Saturday chores ahead of time, I'll see to it that you have the money to go." Come Saturday morning the chores were done and the young boy stood dressed in his Sunday best by the breakfast table. His father reached down in his overalls and pulled out a dollar bill—the most money the boy had ever had at one time in all his life.

The father cautioned him to be careful and then sent him on his way to town. The boy was so excited his feet hardly seemed to touch the ground all the way. When he got to the village, he noticed people were lining the streets and he worked his way through the crowd till he could see what was coming. And there in the distance approached the spectacle of a circus parade.

It was the grandest thing this boy had ever seen. There were tigers and apes in cages and bands and midgets and all that goes to make up a circus parade. After everything had passed by where he was standing, the traditional circus clown, with floppy shoes and baggy pants and brightly painted face, came bringing up the rear.

As the clown passed where he was standing, the boy reached into his pocket and got out that precious dollar bill. Handing the money to the clown, the boy then turned around and went home. What had happened? The boy thought he had seen the circus. But all he had seen was a preview, a glimpse of the wonderful performance that was to come under the big top.[11]

Application: Don't we pass up the real thing for an imitation? Jesus is the real thing.

3rd Sunday

John 2:13–25

Cleansing the Temple

Theme: Anger, which Jesus shows in his concern for the reverence due the temple of God, may be needed to do the work of God.

Billy Martin tells a story about himself and Mickey Mantle in his autobiography, *Number 1*. Billy says he and Mickey Mantle were doing a little hunting down in Texas. Mickey had a friend who would let him hunt on his ranch. When they got there, Mickey told Billy to wait in the car while he went in and cleared things with his friend. Permission was quickly granted for them to hunt, but the owner asked Mickey to do him a favor. He had a pet mule in the barn who was going blind and he didn't have the heart to put him out of his misery. He asked Mickey to shoot the mule for him. Mickey agreed.

On the way back to the car a plan formed in Mantle's mind. Reaching the car, he pretended to be angry. He scowled and slammed the car door shut. Billy wanted to know what was wrong. Mickey replied that the owner wouldn't let them hunt there after all. "I'm so mad at that guy that I'm going out to that barn and shoot one of his mules," Mantle said. He drove like a madman to the barn. Martin protested: "We can't do that!" But Mickey was adamant. "Just watch me," he shouted.

When they got to the barn, Mantle jumped out of the car with his rifle, ran to the barn and shot the mule and killed it. When he got back to the car he saw that Martin had also taken his gun out and smoke was curling from its barrel, too. "What are you doing, Martin?" Mantle yelled. Martin answered, "We'll show that son-of-a-gun. I killed two of his cows."[12]

Application: Are we ever concerned about whether or not our anger is based on God's will?

4th Sunday

John 3:14–21

God So Loved the World

Theme: Loving us so much, God sent the Son to redeem us.

The manager of a ten-story building was informed that a man was trapped in an elevator between the second and third floors. He rushed to the grill work under the stalled car and called to the passenger, "Keep cool, sir; we'll have you out soon. I've phoned for the elevator mechanic." There was a brief pause and a tense voice replied, "I am the elevator mechanic."[13]

Application: We could not have gotten ourselves out of the grip of sin. We are helpless without God.

When the American Civil War was in progress, and when the South had rebelled against the North on the question of slavery, someone once asked Lincoln: "When this war is over, and when the South has been subdued and conquered, and has come back into the Union, how are you gong to treat these rebellious Southerners, what are you going to do to them?" Back came Lincoln's answer: "I am going to treat them as if they had never been away."[14]

Application: God, who is love, forgives us. Do we forgive others?

A minister who had recently lost his wife took his seven-year-old daughter with him to Europe. They were crossing the ocean on a ship, and one of the passengers learned that he was a minister. The captain came to him and asked if he would conduct the Sunday services. "I do not know what denomination you are," the Captain said,"but I wish you would speak on the love of God."

This was a difficult topic for the minister, who was still deep in grief over the loss of his wife. But because he had survived this test of faith, he was able to stand before the people and talk about the immeasurable love of Christ. After lunch he and his daughter were standing on deck, leaning on the railing. The little girl said,

"Daddy, you said that God loves us. How much does [God] love us?" "More than anybody," said the father.

"Daddy, does God love us as much as Mommy loved us?" The father answered yes, then looked out over the ocean. He said, "Look. Look in that direction. God's love extends farther than that." Pointing in the opposite direction over endless miles of ocean, he said, "Look the other way. God's love is greater than that." Pointing at the sky he said, "God's love is taller than that," and down at the ocean, "God's love is deeper than that."

Biting her lip to hold back the tears, the little girl said, "Daddy, isn't it wonderful that we are standing out here in the middle of it?"[15]

Application: God's love is infinite. What limits do we put on our love?

A little boy had gone to the mountains for the first time with his parents. Since this was a camping trip, the boy would wander around the campsite and walk along the winding trails. One day he was standing near an overlook that viewed the deep valley below. He thought he heard a familiar sound and he yelled "Hello." An echo (he had never heard an echo), came back: "Hello." The boy heard this and asked, "Who are you?" And the echo asked, "Who are you?" And the boy cried, "I asked you first." And the voice came back, "I asked you first." Then the boy, in frustration, yelled, "I hate you." The voice came back. "I hate you."

The child ran back to the campsite and told his mother exactly what had happened. The mother talked with him about the echo and told him to go back and do what she instructed him to do. So he went back to the overlook and cried out, "Hello." And immediately he heard from below, "Hello." "I'm sorry," said the lad. "I'm sorry," came back the echo. Then the boy said, "I love you." And he received back the reply, "I love you."[16]

Application: Love begets love. Do we reap love by sowing it?

5th Sunday

John 12:20–33

The Grain of Wheat Must Die

Theme: We must die to ourselves to bear fruit in Christ.

In New Zealand there are more flightless birds than anywhere on earth. Among these are the kiwi and the penguin. Scientists tell us that these birds had wings but lost them. They had no use for them. They had no natural predators on those beautiful islands, and food was plentiful. Since there was no reason to fly, they didn't. Through neglect they lost their wings.

Compare them to the eaglet that somehow ended up in a chicken barnyard. The eaglet was raised with the chickens, pecking at corn and strutting around the chicken coop. One day a mountain man, passing by, recognized the bird, now a fully grown eagle, and asked the farmer if he could work to rehabilitate it. The farmer said, "Go ahead, but it's useless. All that eagle knows is pecking corn like a chicken."

The mountaineer began weeks of rigorous training with the eagle, forcing it to run after him so that it had to use its wings. Many times the eagle fell out of the limbs of trees onto its head. One day, finally, the mountaineer took the eagle to the top of a mountain and held it above his head on his wrist. Giving an upward thrust to his arm, he sent the eagle into the sky with a "Fly!"

The eagle circled and wheeled upward, straining, till soon it took off in a majestic sweep and looked directly into the sun. It was gone. It had regained its nature. It was an eagle once more.[17]

Application: We have the choice of remaining kiwis or penguins, or of going through the pain of becoming the eagles God has called us to be. What is our choice? How do we make decisions?

Passion (Palm) Sunday

Mark 14:1—15:47

The Passion and Death of Jesus
Theme: We join our sufferings to those of Christ . . .
then they make sense.

A.J. Cronin tells of his days as a medical officer to a Welsh mining company in his book *Adventures in Two Worlds*.

I have told you of Olwen Davies, the middle-aged district nurse who for more than twenty years, with fortitude and patience, calmness and cheerfulness, served the people of Tregenny. This unconscious selflessness, which above all seemed the keynote of her character, was so poorly rewarded, it worried me. Although she was much beloved by the people, her salary was most inadequate. And late one night after a particularly strenuous case, I ventured a protest to her as we drank a cup of tea together. "Nurse," I said, "Why don't you make them pay you more? It's ridiculous that you should work for so little." She raised her eyebrows slightly. But she smiled. "I have enough to get along." "No, really," I persisted, "you ought to have an extra pound a week at least. God knows you're worth it." There was a pause. Her smile remained, but her gaze held a gravity, an intensity which startled me. "Doctor," she said, "If God knows I'm worth it, that's all that matters to me."[18]

Application: Are we content to do our work in silence, knowing that God knows our efforts, concerns, sufferings?

Easter

Easter Sunday

John 20:1–9

Resurrection

Theme: Jesus is our salvation.

A good ol' boy made an unusual request for his internment with his funeral director: "I want to be buried in my trusty old pick-up truck." The undertaker tried to talk him out of the bizarre request but to no avail. "It's like this," said the good ol' boy; "I ain't never seen a hole that that old truck couldn't get me out of."[19]

Application: To what extent, concretely, do we rely on Jesus in everyday life?

A woman and her husband had an amusing experience. Their priest had asked her husband, Sam, to do some rewiring in the confessionals. The only way to reach the wiring was to enter the attic above the altar and crawl over the ceiling by balancing on the rafters. Concerned for her husband's safety, Christine waited in a pew. Unbeknown to Christine, some other parishioners were congregating in the vestibule. They paid little attention to her, probably assuming she was praying. Worried about her husband, she looked up toward the ceiling and yelled, "Sam, Sam—are you up there? Did you make it okay?" There was quite an outburst from the vestibule when Sam's hearty voice echoed down, "Yes, I made it up here just fine!"[20]

Application: With Jesus we'll rise and make it up there just fine, too.

Comedian Jerry Clower tells about Uncle Versie Ledbetter who had a mule named Della. One day Della fell in a cistern Uncle

Versie thought he had covered up, but hadn't. Old Della stumbled and fell down in that cistern about thirty feet.

Well, Uncle Versie had a problem. There was his best mule down at the bottom of that cistern and no way he could get the mule out of there. He didn't want her to stay down there and starve to death, and so he decided he would get a shovel and cover her up. It would be cruel but it wouldn't be as cruel and inhumane as to let Della starve to death in the bottom of that deep cistern. Uncle Versie took a shovelful of dirt and threw it down into the cistern. Every time a shovelful of dirt would hit old Della, she'd shake the dirt off and stomp it. Eventually, Della walked on out.[21]

Application: Do we really believe that with Jesus our obstacles can become stepping stones? Do we live in this belief?

2nd Sunday
John 20:19–31

Doubting Thomas
Theme: Jesus turns doubt into an occasion for an increase in faith.

Have you ever watched geese fly in a V-shaped formation? While a thing of beauty to watch, the formation is essential to the geese for survival. If you listen, you can hear the beat of their wings whistling through the air in unison. And that's the secret of their strength: the lead goose cuts a swath through the air resistance, which creates a helping uplift for the birds behind it. In turn, their flapping makes it easier for the birds behind them, and so on. Each bird takes its turn at being the leader. The tired ones fan out to the edges of the V for a breather, and the rested ones surge toward the point of the V to drive the flock onward.

If a goose becomes too exhausted or ill and has to drop out of the flock, it is never abandoned. A stronger member of the flock will follow the failing, weak one to its resting place and wait until the bird is well enough to fly again. Together, cooperating as a flock, geese can fly at a 71-percent longer range, with up to 60 percent less work.[22]

Application: Do we belong to a community of faith in which our faith can be nourished? What steps can we take to foster a faith community?

3rd Sunday
Luke 24:35–48

Risen Jesus Eats Fish
Theme: Jesus' resurrection is the fulfillment of the Old Testament.

A major corporation announced it would be moving its corporate offices across the country. During an interview with the press, the board's chairman was asked if he expected that most of the employees would transfer, but secretaries and others would not. When the secretaries read in the paper the next day that they were not among the "important" employees, they decided to call attention to their importance by not answering phones. The turmoil which resulted from this demonstration of importance caused the board chairman to make a public apology.[23]

Application: In doing the work of Christ, there is no one who is unimportant. We all count.

4th Sunday
John 10:11–18

Good Shepherd
Theme: Jesus shepherds us.

Dr. Martin Luther King wrote: "One night . . . I settled into bed late . . . and just as I was about to doze off the telephone rang. An angry voice on the other end of the line said, 'Listen, nigger, we've taken all we want from you; before next week you'll be sorry you ever came to Montgomery.' I hung up . . . and sleep would not come. It was as if all my fears coalesced into one giant terror. I got out of bed and began to walk the floor.

"Finally I went to the kitchen and made a pot of coffee. I was ready to give up. With my cup of coffee sitting untouched before me, I tried to think of a way to move out of the picture without

appearing a coward. In this state of exhaustion I decided to take
my problem to God.

"With my head in my hands, I bowed over the kitchen table
and prayed aloud. The words I spoke to God that midnight are
still vivid in my memory. 'Lord, I am here taking a stand for what
I believe is right. But now I'm afraid. The people are looking to
me for leadership, and if I do not stand before them with strength
and courage, they also will falter. I am at the end of my powers. I
have nothing left. I can't face it alone.'

"At that moment I experienced the presence of God as I had
never experienced [God] before. It seemed I heard the quiet assurance of [God's] voice saying: 'Stand up for righteousness,
stand up for truth; and I will be at your side.' My fears evaporat-
ed and my uncertainty disappeared. I was ready to follow [God]
and face anything."[24]

*Application: If necessary, the shepherd is ready to die for his sheep. To
what extent are we willing to put ourselves out for others?*

5th Sunday
John 15:1–8

Vine and the Branches
*Theme: We remain alive spiritually by remaining in Jesus,
who is our life.*

A missionary in Africa lived in his central mission which had a
small electric plant to supply current for his church and small rec-
tory. Some natives from an outlying mission came to visit the pa-
dre. They noticed the electric light hanging from the ceiling of his
living room. They watched wide-eyed as he turned the little
switch and the light went on.

One of the visitors asked if he could have one of those bulbs.
The priest, thinking he wanted it for a sort of trinket or bauble,
gave him a burned-out bulb. On his next visit to the outlying mission the priest stopped at the hut of the man who had asked for
the bulb. Imagine the priest's surprise when he saw the bulb
hanging from an ordinary string. He had to explain that one had

to have electricity and a wire to bring the current to the bulb.[25]

Application: How do we understand the statement that without Jesus we can do nothing?

6th Sunday

John 15:9–17

New Commandment of Love
Theme: All Scripture is summed up in Jesus' commandment of love.

A young woman walked into a fabric shop and asked the proprietor if she had any kind of noisy, rustling material in white. The proprietor searched the inventory and finally found two bolts of fabric that fit the description. As she was cutting the fabric to the customer's specifications, the proprietor's curiosity got the best of her and she asked why the woman wanted such an unusual and noisy cloth. The young woman replied, "You see, I'm making a wedding gown, and my fiancé is blind. When I walk down the aisle, I want him to know when I've arrived at the altar, so he won't be embarrassed."[26]

Application: Love, which finds all kinds of ways to express itself, is willing to sacrifice for the beloved. What time limits do we place on our sacrifice for family members? For friends? For strangers?

7th Sunday

John 17:11–19

Jesus Prays His Followers May Be One
Theme: Prayer is necessary if we are to be united with Jesus and one another.

A cross-country bus made a scheduled stop at a depot that was located near four different restaurants. The driver announced, "Folks, we'll be here for thirty minutes. The bus line has a strict policy never to recommend an eating place by name, so I am not permitted to tell you which restaurant of the four you have to choose from here is the best. However, I can say this. While we are here, if any of you should need me for any reason, I'll be at Tony's Diner directly across the street."[27]

Application: Our actions tell people what our true beliefs are. Do our actions help build up the Body of Christ?

Pentecost
John 20:19–23

Receive the Holy Spirit
Theme: The Holy Spirit infuses us with power.

A tanker was beached on shore. All day efforts had been made to return the huge vessel to the water, but with no success. Finally the captain told all crews and companies to stop; he went to his cabin and waited. When the tide came in that night the waters lifted the thousand-ton tanker off the beach and carried it, light as a feather, back into the deep.[28]

Application: In what ways do we expect the Holy Spirit to be revealed in our life?

Holy Trinity
Matthew 28:16–20

Jesus' Great Commission
*Theme: Jesus sends us to preach the Father,
Son and Spirit to all nations.*

A family was hosting an eleven-year-old girl from India. The Hindu girl decided on her own to go with the family to Sunday Mass. When they came home, the husband asked the girl how she liked the Mass. "I don't understand why the West Coast isn't included, too," the girl replied. When they inquired what she meant, she said, "You know, in the name of the Father, and of the Son, and of the whole East Coast."[29]

Application: Does our apostolic concern extend to all people, either by action or by prayer?

Corpus Christi

Mark 14:12–16, 22–26

The Last Supper
Theme: Jesus comes to us in the Holy Eucharist.

In the Vietnam War, some stray artillery rounds landed in an orphanage, wounding several children. One was a nine-year-old girl who lost a lot of blood. Word quickly reached nearby American forces and they dispatched a Navy doctor and nurse to help the children. They went to work first on the young girl who was in shock and needed an immediate blood transfusion to save her life.

To get a donor, the doctor and nurse called together a group of the unharmed children, and in their stumbling Vietnamese and limited French they explained to the orphans that someone would have to give blood to help save the little girl's life. At first nothing but silence and stares came from the frightened youngsters. Then a small hand went up in jumpy hesitation, then down again, then up again, the hand of a little boy, age ten.

The nurse quickly asked his name. "Heng," he replied in a whisper. He was placed on a cot; his blood quickly drawn for a compatibility test, which it passed; then the transfusion started from him to the little girl. But Heng soon broke into crying that grew into deep sobs. "Is it hurting, Heng?" asked the nurse. He shook his head no, but went into deeper sobs and began to shake. Soon he was into a flood of tears. The medical team became nervous. Something was wrong.

At that moment a Vietnamese nurse arrived on the scene. She quickly spoke to Heng in his own language, engaging him in rapid-fire dialogue. After answering several sobbing questions, she whispered softly to him. Then he became calm and his crying faded away. Turning to the American medics, the nurse said in subdued tones: "He thought he was going to die. He had the impression that you needed all his blood, and that he would have to die to help save the little girl's life."

The shocked doctor asked, "How could he possibly have the guts to do that?" The Vietnamese nurse turned and asked the little fellow. He answered simply, "Because she is my friend."[30]

Application: Jesus has given himself to us. In what ways do we give ourselves to others?

═══ Ordinary Time ═══

2nd Sunday
John 1:35–42

Two Disciples Follow Jesus
Theme: We are called to follow Jesus, as the apostles were.

A company advertised an opening in its sales force. It received more than 1000 applications for the job. But of those many letters and resumes, one letter stood out: "I am presently selling furniture at the address below. You may judge my ability as a salesman if you will stop in to see me any time, pretending that you are interested in buying furniture.

"When you come in, you can identify me by my red hair. I will have no way of identifying you. That way, the sales abilities I exhibit will be no more than my usual everyday approach and not a special effort to impress a potential employer." The sales manager took the applicant up on his challenge and visited the furniture store. You won't be surprised to learn that the redhead got the job.[31]

Application: Jesus is looking for a few good men and women. How enthusiastic is our response to his call?

3rd Sunday
Mark 1:14–20

Andrew and Peter Follow Jesus
Theme: We are called to make a radical decision: to be disciples of Jesus.

Perhaps we can apply to ourselves a cartoon about Calvin. Walking along life's road one day, Calvin, the boy wonder of comic fame, says to his faithful tiger, Hobbes: "Mom and Dad say I should make my life an example of the principles I believe in."

Walking a bit further, he continues: "But every time I do, they tell me to stop it." Hobbes responds: "I'm not sure that total self-indulgence is really a principle."[32]

Application: Is our decision to follow Jesus a total commitment?

4th Sunday
Mark 1:21–28

Jesus Casts Out Devils
Theme: Authority comes from within, from a life with God.

Authority is a strange thing. A fourteen-year-old boy argues about the curfew imposed by his parents. Then the next day in the freshman baseball game, he dutifully lays down a good bunt, foregoing a mighty swing for the fence, because the coach flashed a signal from the bench. Instant obedience to the coach; reluctant submission to mom and dad. On an airliner the captain flashes the seat belt sign and everybody complies. Four hours later in a rented car, the passenger disregards the seat belt. The irony: for the same distance traveled, the airliner is three times safer.[33]

Application: Do we see authority and humility as walking together in daily life?

5th Sunday
Mark 1:29–39

Peter's Mother-in-Law Is Healed
Theme: Faith is necessary for healing.

Hauling clay for a landfill, a truck driver backed his dump truck too far over the grade. The weight of his load lifted the front end of the truck several feet off the ground. "Now what are you going to do?" asked his helper. Easing from the cab, the driver said, "I think I'll grease it. I'll never get a better chance." Now there's a man with a lot of faith![34]

Application: If we pray in faith for God to heal us—physically, psychologically—do we expect to be healed? If not, why not?

6th Sunday

Mark 1:40–45

Jesus Heals the Leper
Theme: Jesus wants to heal us.

Chad Varah was an Anglican priest. In 1953 he buried a girl of 18 who had killed herself. The coroner, at her inquest, suggested that she might not have done this desperate act if someone had been around who would have listened to her troubles. Chad Varah decided to use his London church and a telephone to listen to people who were in despair. He put a small advertisement in the local paper, and during the first week he had 27 calls.

Soon he was listening and advising people 12 hours each day. There were so many people waiting in his outer office to see him that he asked some of his congregation to come and provide cups of tea for them. Then he found that often people who had come into the outer office in great distress had become different people by the time they reached him, and some did not even wait to see him because one of the helpers had befriended them.

So he decided to train a group of his congregation so that they could be more helpful in the way they befriended the clients. That is how the Samaritans were formed.[35]

Application: We heal as Jesus did: by our loving care for others. Do we try to be sensitive to the suffering of others?

7th Sunday

Mark 2:1–12

Jesus Heals the Paralytic
Theme: No one was excluded from Jesus' love.

Once upon a time, there were some animals on a farm who got into an argument over who was the most valuable. The cow argued that she was because she gave the farmer her milk. The sheep said no, he was because he gave the farmer his wool. The chicken clucked and said, "That's ridiculous. How would the farmer have breakfast if not for my eggs?" Even the cat got into the conversation. "Think how much grain the farmer would lose if I didn't kill the mice," he said.

While the animals were arguing over who was the most important, the little puppy dog was over in the corner feeling very sorry for himself. "I guess I am not very valuable at all," he said to himself. "I don't give milk, or wool, or eggs, or even catch mice. I am no good at all."

What the little puppy dog didn't know was that the farmer loved the little puppy dog most of all. Why do you suppose that was? That's right. When the farmer came to the house after a long day in the field, the little dog ran out with his tail wagging and barking joy. The farmer would reach down and pick the puppy up in his arms and the puppy would happily lick his face. What the puppy knew how to give better than any of the other animals was his love.[36]

Application: All of us, even the seemingly unimportant, have much love to give and deserve our love. Is there someone, or a group, that we exclude from our love?

8th Sunday
Mark 2:18–22

New Wine, Old Wineskins
Theme: Jesus, in coming, fulfills the Old Testament and inaugurates the New Covenant.

People in a centuries-old basilica in Turkey had the habit of coming in and bowing to the back wall of the spacious church. No one knew why people did this, since the main altar was at the other end of the cathedral. Then it was decided to renovate the beautiful old church. The renovation was done by an art expert, for authorities suspected that beautiful paintings were beneath the drab exterior of some of the walls.

Sure enough, when the back wall was uncovered by removing layers of plaster and paint, an exquisitely beautiful painting of the Madonna was found. Further study found that people centuries ago had always bowed to the painting out of deep reverence. Although the painting had been covered over in centuries of occupation by pagan forces, its beauty was undiminished when restored . . . and the reason for people bowing to a supposed blank wall was also uncovered.[37]

Application: Traditions are helpful only if we know why we keep them and if they continue to promote good. What traditions no longer speak to us? Why do we hang on to those that have become meaningless?

9th Sunday

Mark 2:23—3:6

Jesus Reveals Hypocrisy
Theme: Jesus wants mercy rather than sacrifice.

The old shoemaker was tired. He wanted to die and go be with the Lord. Or at least, he would like the Lord to visit him. One day he thought he heard a voice in his prayer. The voice said, "Tomorrow I will come to your shop." Overjoyed, the cobbler went to work, fully expecting to see the Lord. But as the day went on, nothing out of the ordinary happened.

An old woman came in complaining about some boys who were stealing her apples. Since he knew the boys, the cobbler called them in and talked with them. The boys said they would stop. The old woman was pleased.

Then a fellow down on his luck came in. He needed a meal. The cobbler told him about the Mission in the city. But the fellow was not acquainted with the town. So the cobbler walked him there. Hurrying back, the cobbler waited for the Lord.

Late in the day, a girl came in. He knew her. She said her father was sick and needed help. The cobbler again left his work and went with the girl to get a doctor for her father. Late in the day, the cobbler returned to his shop. He closed it down, sad. The Lord had not come. He went to his room for his hour of prayer.

"Lord," he prayed, "I'm sorry I was out of the shop so much today, so busy. I hope you did not come when I was away." Then
he heard a voice: "I came to you in each person you helped. You
did enjoy my presence. I am very pleased with you."[38]

*Application: Do we believe that Jesus comes to us in others? If so, how
does this belief change our life?*

10th Sunday

Mark 3:20–35

Jesus Casts Out Devils
*Theme: We must follow the Spirit's lead, even though others may think
we're fools.*

Newspaper columnist George Plagenz once told the story of a
young doctor who delivered a baby into a poverty-stricken family
in Montana. The child had one cruelly deformed leg. He also had
difficulty breathing. "The other children will call him 'Limpy,'"
the doctor thought. "His life will be miserable. If I don't do anything for his breathing, he will die. Wouldn't that be better?" he
asked himself. Then he remembered his Hippocratic oath and began blowing into the baby's mouth. Soon the child's lungs were
acting normally and he gave his first cry.

Several years later the doctor's daughter and son-in-law were
killed in an auto accident. The doctor's ten-year-old granddaughter was left an orphan. He took her in. One day the child
was stricken with a crippling and incurable condition. The doctor
learned there was a young doctor in the Midwest who had been
getting excellent results in the treatment of this particular disease.
He took his granddaughter to see the doctor.

The young physician was lame. He was the deformed baby
into whose mouth the older doctor had breathed 35 years before.
Because of his own infirmity, the young doctor had specialized in
this crippling disease. The treatment on the older doctor's grand-
child was successful and the little girl was returned to normal
health.[39]

Application: God can draw straight with crooked lines. Are we trusting enough and foolish enough to act on this belief?

11th Sunday

Mark 4:26–34

The Power of the Seed
Theme: Faith is a powerful seed.

One of the strangest seeds in the world is the seed of the Chinese bamboo tree. It lies buried in the soil for five years before any seedling or sprout appears above ground. Think of it! Five years! All during these five years the seed must be cultivated, that is, watered and fertilized regularly. Now comes the big surprise.

When the bamboo seedling finally emerges from the ground, it grows to a height of nine feet in just six weeks. Why does the seedling take so long to emerge? Why does it grow so fast once it emerges? Plant experts say that during its first five years in the soil the bamboo seed is busy building an elaborate root system. It's this root system that enables it to grow nine feet in six weeks.[40]

Application: Does our faith have deep roots? How can we know? What is our root system that nourishes us spiritually every day?

12th Sunday

Mark 4:35–41

Jesus Walks on Stormy Seas
Theme: Faith bolsters peace in our life.

Our age has some techniques for relaxation. On a beautiful day in the park a young father was pushing his screaming child in his stroller. As the father wheeled his infant son along the path, he kept murmuring, "Easy now, Donald. Just keep calm, Donald. It's all right, Donald. Just relax, Donald. It's gonna be all right, Donald . . ."

A woman passing by said to the young father, "You certainly

know how to talk to an upset child—quietly and gently." The women then leaned over the stroller and cooed, "What seems to be the trouble, Donald?" The father said quickly, "Oh, no . . . He's Henry. I'm Donald!"[41]

Application: In times of unrest or crisis, do we pray in faith?

13th Sunday
Mark 5:21–43

Jairus's Daughter
Theme: Jesus wants us to respond in faith to life's problems.

John Killinger tells a moving story about a couple whose newborn son was mentally retarded. They were crushed, of course. Still, they loved him as they would any child of theirs. They built a bedroom with glass walls so that wherever they were in the house they would be able to keep an eye on him. For seventeen years, the mother slept next to the boy with her hand next to his heart. If he ever started having trouble breathing, she would be able to wake up and give him artificial respiration. For seventeen years, they lived this way.

One sad day, however, a neighbor's girl fell from a tree and hurt her arm. The mother left her son to rush the girl to a hospital. As she was standing in the emergency room of the hospital with the little girl, her husband came in carrying the body of their son. He had died while she was at the hospital. His father had tried vainly to revive him. As the boy lay before them in peace, the parents wept. But then they gave thanks to God for the gift of their son. "For," his mother said, "he taught us how to love."[42]

Application: Learning to love is the greatest healing that faith can bring about. Have we been healed in this way?

14th Sunday

Mark 6:1–6

Jesus Rejected by His Hometown
Theme: We will suffer rejection in witnessing for Jesus.

In 1960 a religious persecution broke out in the territory of Sudan in Africa. A Christian black student named Paride Taban fled the danger and went to Uganda. While in Uganda, he studied for the priesthood and was ordained. When things settled down in Sudan, young Fr. Taban returned to his homeland. He was assigned to a parish in Palotaka.

But his African congregation found it hard to believe that he was really a priest. Fr. Taban says: "The people looked hard at me and asked, 'Do you mean to say, black man, that you are a priest? We can't believe it.'" These people had never had a black priest before. They had always had white priests who gave them clothing and medicine. Young Fr. Taban was from the Madi tribe and had nothing to give them. He was poor like them. To make matters worse, Fr. Taban had to introduce them to the changes of the Second Vatican Council.

These changes bothered the people greatly. They said to one another: "This young black man turns our altar around and celebrates Mass in our own language. He cannot be a real priest." Only after a great deal of difficulty did the people of Palotaka finally accept Fr. Taban.[43]

Application: If we try to live "in Jesus," we will be rejected as he was. Do we turn to Jesus when we encounter rejection?

15th Sunday

Mark 6:7–13

Jesus Sends Apostles Out on Mission
Theme: We must be detached to give ourselves completely to the Lord.

We can become like the dog in a large crate on the platform of a railroad station. He was the saddest dog you can imagine. A lady asked about him. "You would be sad, too," she was told, "if you were in his plight. He's chewed the tag off the crate, and doesn't know where he's going."[44]

Application: What is the specific mission Jesus has called us to?

16th Sunday
Mark 6:30–34

Jesus Takes His Apostles Aside to Rest
Theme: Jesus wants us to rest in him, as we also spend ourselves for him.

Judson Swihart once put it like this: "Some people are like medieval castles. Their high walls keep them safe from being hurt. They protect themselves emotionally by permitting no exchange of feelings with others. No one can enter. They are secure from attack. However, inspection of the occupant finds him or her lonely, rattling around his castle alone. The castle dweller is a self-made prisoner. He or she needs to feel loved by someone, but the walls are so high that it is difficult to reach out or for anyone else to reach in."[45]

Application: To find Jesus, we must let others in. Do we have a community of faith in which we can seek, find, and rest in Jesus?

17th Sunday
John 6:1–15

Multiplication of Loaves and Fishes
Theme: Jesus gives us his Body and Blood to nourish us.

Two fellows died recently and were walking the golden streets of God's celestial realm. There was more beauty and more splendor and more joy there than they had ever dreamed imaginable. One of them turned to the other and said, "Isn't this wonderful?" The other replied, "Yes, and to think we could have gotten here ten years sooner if we hadn't eaten all that oat bran."[46]

Application: How, in everyday life, do we help others?

18th Sunday

John 6:24–35

Jesus, Our Imperishable Food
Theme: The Eucharist and faith each enrich the other.

A farmer brought a load of wheat to the elevator in a nearby town. He stopped at a restaurant and sat down near a group of young fellows who were acting up, shouting at the cook, and heckling the waitress. When his meal was set before him, the old gentleman bowed his head to offer a prayer. One of the smart-alecks thought he would have some fun with the farmer, so he shouted in a voice that could be heard by everyone: "Hey, Pop, does everyone do that where you come from?" Calmly the old man turned toward the lad and in an equally loud voice replied: "No, son, the pigs don't."[47]

Application: Do we nourish our faith life with the Eucharist on a regular basis?

19th Sunday

John 6:41–51

Living Bread
Theme: Jesus is our Bread of Life, our spiritual nourishment.

A certain minister was disturbed to see a shabby old man go into his church at noon every day and come out again after a few minutes. What could he be doing? He informed the caretaker and asked him to question the man. After all, the place contained valuable furnishings. "I go to pray," the old man said in reply to the caretaker's questioning. "Come on," said the other, "you are never long enough in the church to pray." "Well, you see," the shabby old man went on, "I cannot pray a long prayer, but every day at 12 o'clock, I just come in and say, 'Jesus, it's Jim,' and wait a minute and then come away. It's just a little prayer, but I guess He hears me."

When Jim was injured some time later and taken to the hospital, he had a wonderful influence in the ward. Grumbling patients became cheerful and often the ward would ring with laughter. "Well, Jim," said the sister to him one day, "the men say you are responsible for this change in the ward. They say you are always happy."

"Yes, sister, I am. I can't help being happy. You see, it's my visitor. Every day he makes me happy."

"Your visitor?" The sister was puzzled. She noticed that Jim's chair was always empty on visiting days, for he was a lonely old man, with no relations. "Your visitor? But when does he come?"

"Every day," Jim replied, the light in his eyes growing brighter. "Yes, every day at 12 o'clock he comes and stands at the foot of my bed. I see him and he smiles and says, 'Jim, it's Jesus.'"[48]

Application: Jesus can be with us in many ways. Do we see Jesus in others as well as in the Eucharist?

20th Sunday
John 6:51–58

Eat My Body—Drink My Blood
Theme: The Eucharist can make us one.

During the Second World War a group of GI's found themselves in the square of a French village. No one was around. They were tired and hungry. The people were hiding behind their shutters, unaware that the Allies had the Nazis on the run. A GI spotted one timid citizen behind a pillar: "Do you know where we can get something to eat?" The man shrunk back further. The GI turned to his companion and said, "Guess we'll just have to make some 'Stone Soup.'"

A few windows went up farther to listen to and observe this "Stone Soup." The two GI's gathered some kindling and sticks and soon had a roaring fire going in the town square. A small crowd started to gather. "Anyone got a pot or kettle?" Someone bought a large pot. The GI's found some water and filled the pot, stirring it vigorously. "Sure wish we had some potatoes," one GI said. A man went off and brought back some potatoes. The GI's stirred the pot vigorously.

The crowd was now quite large. "Some carrots, beets, and onions would really be nice." These items mysteriously materialized from dark cellar caches. By now the aroma of the stew was spreading throughout the village and almost everyone was in the town square. Someone brought some meat to throw in the pot. Soon two accordions appeared. "Time to eat!" cried one GI. He began to ladle up the rich, juicy hot stew and hand it out to the townspeople, who were hungry too.

After everyone had eaten, the music and dancing continued till morning. Soon the people went back to their house. But everyone said the "Stone Soup" was the nicest meal they had ever had.[49]

Application: The Eucharist is "stone soup," life-giving food for our spirits. How important do we regard the celebration of the Eucharist?

21st Sunday

John 6:60–69

Some Disciples Leave Jesus
Theme: We must decide for or against the eucharistic Jesus.

During the Second World War certain Nazis killed some Jews and buried them in a mass grave. One twelve-year-old boy was still alive. He dug his way out of the shallow dirt and went around the neighborhood seeking shelter in homes. The people knew what had happened and, when they saw the boy caked with dirt, they hurriedly shut the door in his face. One [woman] was about to do the same when the boy said: "Lady, don't you recognize me? I'm the Jesus you Christians say you love." The lady broke into tears and received the boy into her home. She had made her decision for Jesus.[50]

Application: The Eucharist calls us to decide: are we for Jesus or not?

22nd Sunday

Mark 7:1–8,14–15,21–23

Jesus Accuses Pharisees of Hypocrisy

*Theme: Jesus wants our words and deeds
to spring from a life lived in him.*

A visitor to Poland was being shown around [during Communist times] by a party official. The visitor said, "Are you Catholic?" and the official answered, "Believing, but not practicing." The visitor later asked, "Are you a communist?" The official smiled and said, "Practicing, but not believing."[51]

Application: Are our words and actions as disciples of Jesus consistent with our belief in him?

23rd Sunday

Mark 7:31–37

Jesus Heals Deaf and Dumb Man

Theme: Jesus may heal us slowly to elicit our faithful cooperation.

The need to be listened to is great. The chaplain at a state mental hospital told of the sad case of a Greek man in an institution who was thought to be a hopeless schizophrenic. The man had been vegetating in the hospital for years. No one knew much about him, where he had come from, but all agreed he was a hopeless case. The chaplain asked the Greek Orthodox priest in the community to pay the man a visit, just to give the poor fellow a chance to speak in his native tongue as much as for any pastoral reasons. He hadn't had a chance to do this for years.

The Greek Orthodox priest returned from the visit and asked the chaplain: "What in the world is that fellow doing there? He's as healthy as you and I." Bit by bit the tragic story unfolded.

The Greek had jumped ship long ago in a nearby port. Speaking no English, he had gotten into some sort of trouble and as mistakes sometimes happen, he was locked up in a mental institution. There he slowly learned English, but he learned his English from schizophrenic patients.

Certain language misuse is characteristic of that mental dysfunction, and the poor Greek fellow managed to learn totally schizophrenic English. To all English personnel he sounded schizophrenic and as removed from reality as his fellow patients. The priest, however, conversed with him in Greek, the first time anyone had done that in the hospital, and the man spoke perfectly correct Greek. The hospital staff were humbled and were taught a lesson by the experience.[52]

Application: Spending time to understand others can go a long way toward healing them—and us. Do we try to understand the viewpoint and feelings of others?

24th Sunday
Mark 8:27–35
Jesus Predicts His Passion, Rebukes Peter
Theme: Honesty in our relationships,
especially with Jesus, is essential.

The film, *Mother Teresa*, shows her looking over a house being prepared for the nuns in San Francisco. A priest narrates, "I was gently informed that the springs could go, the mattresses could go, the carpeting . . ." A workman then explains the workings of the building's hot water heater, and the nun lightly tells him, "I don't think we will be needing it. For us to be able to understand the poor, we must know what poverty is."[53]

Application: Mother Teresa's simplicity and embrace of poverty are a rebuke to the world. She doesn't play games. How about us?

25th Sunday
Mark 9:30–37
Jesus Predicts Passion, Embraces Child
Theme: Jesus, gentle to children, bore the cross.

Dr. Charles Mayo with his father and brother founded the world-famous Mayo Clinic in Rochester, Minnesota. One time a group of

European medical experts were guests of Dr. Mayo at his home. According to the custom of their homelands the guests placed their shoes outside their bedroom doors to be polished during the night. Dr. Charles was the last to retire. As he went to his room he noticed the shoes. It was too late to wake up any of the servants. With a sigh he gathered up all the footwear, hauled them into the kitchen, and spent half the night polishing them.[54]

Application: Childlikeness and resolute commitment: do we have them both?

26th Sunday

Mark 9:38–43,45,47–48

Jesus Rebukes Apostles for Self-Righteousness
Theme: Our status as disciples lies in doing the will of Jesus.

Each day a king sat in state hearing petitions and dispensing justice. Each day a holy man, dressed in the robe of a poor beggar, approached the king, and silently offered him a piece of a very ripe fruit. Each day the king accepted the fruit, and handed it to his treasurer who stood behind the throne. Each day the beggar, again without a word, withdrew and vanished into the crowd. Year after year this ritual occurred daily.

Then one day, ten years after the beggar first appeared, something different happened. A tame monkey, having escaped from the women's apartments in the inner palace, came bounding into the hall and leapt up onto the arms of the king's throne. The poor beggar had just presented the king with his usual gift. But this time, instead of passing it on to his treasurer as was his usual custom, the king handed it over to the monkey.

When the animal bit into it, a precious jewel dropped out and fell to the floor. The King, amazed, quickly turned to his treasurer behind him. "What has become of all the others?" he asked. But the treasurer had no answer. Over all the years he had simply thrown the unimpressive gifts through a small upper window. He hadn't even unlocked the door. So he excused himself and ran quickly down the stairs and opened up the courtyard. There, on the floor, lay a mass of rotten fruit in various stages of decay. But amidst this garbage of many years lay a heap of precious jewels.[55]

Application: Do we neglect God's gifts in everyday life?

27th Sunday

Mark 10:2–16

Jesus Speaks of Divorce
Theme: Our relationship with God and our spouse requires childlike honesty.

They returned home happy but tired after celebrating their fortieth wedding anniversary with their children and friends. Before falling into bed he offered to make a late-night snack for both of them.

While she slumped into a stool along the kitchen counter, he collected the ham, cheese, and mustard from the refrigerator. Reaching into the breadbox, he took out what turned out to be the last four slices of bread. He carefully made two sandwiches and cut each in quarters, the way she liked them. He placed one of the sandwiches on a plate and placed it in front of her. "How come you always give me the sandwich with the heel of the bread," she said. "Forty years we've been married and you always give me the heel of the bread. I know I've never said anything before, but, honey, I really hate the heel of the bread." Embarrassed, he shrugged his shoulders and said, "I always give you the heel of the bread because it's my favorite piece."

This story shows a tender love. It might also show some lack of communication if, after forty years, the husband didn't know his wife disliked the heel.[56]

Application: How do we communicate with our spouse, our children, neighbors, strangers?

28th Sunday

Mark 10:17–30

Rich Young Man
Theme: Jesus asks for total commitment.

Robert Schuller once asked Coretta Scott King where she got the dream that kept her going. Mrs. King responded, "It was while I was attending Antioch College. . . .I heard a quotation that deeply motivated me. Horace Mann said to his first graduating class at Antioch in the late 1850s, 'Be ashamed to die until you've won some victory for humanity.'"[57]

Application: What is the central motivating factor in our life?

29th Sunday

Mark 10:35–45

John and James Ask for Places of Honor
Theme: Discipleship consists in humble service.

In the best tradition of John Wayne, Rambo, General Patton, Joe Namath, and Henry Kissinger, Archie Bunker has a need to win. It seems Archie discovered that Edith had been letting him win at Monopoly. When the cat is out of the bag, Edith says, "Well, Archie, I thought it would make you feel better if I let you win." At that point, Archie explodes: "Let me win? That'll be the day when I can't win without you letting me win. You spoiled the whole thing. From now on if you want to do something together, do it by yourself!"[58]

Application: Are we inclined always to have things our way, and not focus on serving others?

30th Sunday

Mark 10:46–52

Jesus Heals a Blind Man

Theme: Jesus responds to impetuous, confident faith.

Mrs. Botnick and Mrs. Krasnitz had not visited for some time. "Tell me," asked Mrs. Botnick, "How is your son?"

"Oh, my son—what misfortune!" Mrs. Krasnitz wailed. "He married a girl who doesn't lift a finger around the house. She can't cook, she can't sew a button on a shirt, she can't keep a job; all she does is sleep late. My poor boy brings her breakfast in bed, and all day long she stays in bed, loafing . . ."

"How terrible," Mrs. Botnick said.

"So tell me," Mrs. Krasnitz asked her friend, "how is your daughter?"

"Ah, my daughter!" Mrs. Botnick beamed. "She married a wonderful man, an absolute angel! He won't let her set foot in the kitchen and insists that she not work. He's given her a full-time maid, a cook, and every morning he brings her breakfast in bed! And he makes her stay in bed all day!"[59]

Application: Does our faith prompt us to rejoice in the good fortune of others?

31st Sunday

Mark 12:28–34

Jesus' Great Commandment of Love

Theme: Love must be the center of our life.

When Carpenter, the artist who painted Lincoln's portrait in the White House, asked about his religion, Lincoln replied: "I have never joined any church, but when any church will inscribe over its altar as its sole qualification for membership, the words of the Savior, 'Thou shalt love the Lord thy God with all thy heart and with all thy soul, and thy neighbor as thyself,' that church will I join with all my heart and all my soul."[60]

Application: Is love in action your personal "greatest commandment"? How so?

32nd Sunday

Mark 12:38–44

Widow's Mite

Theme: Jesus praised those who give of the little they have, trusting in God.

You may have heard the story of God's juggler. In the Middle Ages a juggler was juggling his colored balls and pins in the marketplace when some monks came by. The juggler expressed his desire to be a monk. The monks said, "What can you do?" The juggler said, "I juggle." The monks said, "Well, you will have to change your ways."

The juggler became Brother Lawrence in the monastery. Years passed and one Christmas the monks decided that each one would present a masterpiece to the infant Jesus. All but Lawrence came up with an idea. But on Christmas Eve Lawrence locked himself in the church. The monks thought he had gone mad. They ran up to the choir loft and looked down. There was Lawrence juggling before the crib scene. They were going to go down and seize him as berserk. But as Lawrence finished his juggling, the monks saw the infant in the manger reach out with a smile. Lawrence had given his all.[61]

Application: Do we offer our little to God, trusting God to care for us?

33rd Sunday

Mark 13:24–32

End Times

Theme: We must prepare for the end times.

Jimmy was about ten years old. A gang of teenagers gave him a lot of trouble: they pushed him off the sidewalk, tripped him in the schoolyard, and even stole his lunch money. For fear they would give him a beating or cut him with the knife they flashed, Jimmy never told anyone. One day this gang of punks got especially rough. Jimmy blurted out: "I'm going to tell my big brother on you." They sneered: "Bring him on. The bigger they are, the harder they fall."

Several days later the gang saw Jimmy coming down the street, walking beside a husky six-footer dressed in an army uniform with several rows of service ribbons. It was Jimmy's big brother Bob, just returned from Vietnam. Suddenly Bob demanded: "Okay, you little punks, give him the money you took." They emptied their pockets and then promised to get the rest of the stolen money.[62]

Application: Do we think about our death? We prepare for a happy death by walking with Jesus every day.

Christ the King
John 18:33–37

Jesus Before Pilate
Theme: Like Jesus, we must be committed to the truth.

Beneath the picture of a macho-looking Christ runs this message: "Jesus, also known as Christ, wanted on charges of sedition, criminal anarchy, vagrancy, and conspiring to overthrow the established government. Dresses poorly. Uses carpentry as a cover. Has visionary ideas. Associates with common working people, unemployed, and winos. Has variety of aliases: Prince of Peace, Son of Man, Light of the World, etc. Full beard and scars on hands and feet the results of injuries inflicted by angry mob led by respectable citizens and local authorities."[63]

Application: Would we accept Jesus if he were on Main Street today?

Year C

Advent

1st Sunday

Luke 21:25–28,34–36

Being on Guard
Theme: Jesus warns us to watch.

A Sunday school teacher went to a bookstore to get a book on "the rapture," a term for the end times used much by Pentecostalists. His students wanted to know more about the subject. He couldn't remember the title. After hearing the teacher's explanation of the book, the clerk said, "Oh, you must mean, *Eighty-Eight Reasons Why the Rapture Will Definitely Come in 1992.*"

"That sounds like it," the teacher said.

"That also came in a 1993 edition," the clerk said. "We sent back our unsold copies last spring."

The teacher smiled, fully understanding the lack of market value in a book predicting the world's end some years after the vaunted date.[1]

Application: "False prophets will come, deceiving many . . ." Are we critical judges of a good and false prophet?

2nd Sunday

Luke 3:1–6

Voice Crying in the Wilderness
Theme: God calls us to repentance and forgiveness.

A Pearl Harbor TV story is about a veteran who now works in the memorial built over the sunken ship Arizona. He saw a man coming through the memorial thumping his chest and saying, "I am Japanese." The American vet thought he was going to have some trouble with the individual. But the Japanese man came up to the

American vet, put one arm on the American vet's shoulder and said, "I'm sorry." Then he put his other arm on the American vet's other shoulder and said, "I'm so very sorry," and he embraced the American vet in a bear hug and wept. The man's wife came up from her deep bow and she was weeping. The American vet wept as did many standing nearby. They recognized the scene as a healing one for two warriors who had carried many emotions around for years.[2]

Application: What old wounds have we recently tried to heal by reaching out to another and offering forgiveness or asking to be forgiven?

3rd Sunday
Luke 3:10–18

John Preaches Justice
Theme: John calls his generation to prepare for the Messiah's coming.

Dr. Karl Menninger, psychiatrist, wrote a book called *Whatever Became of Sin?* He tells this story: One sunny day in September 1972, a street preacher appeared on a busy corner in downtown Chicago. As office workers hurried by on their way to lunch, the street preacher would suddenly raise his right arm, point a bony finger at an office worker, and shout, "Guilty!" "The effect on the pedestrians was almost eerie," said Dr. Menninger. They would glance at the preacher, look away, glance back, and then hurry on.[3]

Application: Would we feel guilty if this preacher pointed at us? For what?

4th Sunday
Luke 1:39–45

Mary and Elizabeth
Theme: God asked to take his place as a human being in Mary.

A king who had no sons to succeed him posted a sign inviting young men in his kingdom to become his adopted son and rule after him. There were only two qualifications. The boy must love God and neighbor deeply. A young peasant boy felt moved to apply, but he lacked decent clothes for the interview. Finally, he saved enough money for the clothes. As the boy neared the palace, he came upon a shivering old man begging for clothes. The boy was moved to pity and gave the beggar the clothes he had brought for the interview. Then the boy went on to the castle, wondering if he would be admitted in rags. The boy did gain admittance. When he came to the throne room, he couldn't believe his eyes. On the throne sat the shivering old man. The king smiled and said, "Welcome, my son."[4]

Application: God is to be found in everyday life. Do we have trouble seeing God in daily life?

The Birth of the Lord

John 1:1–18

Jesus Comes to Share Our Life

Theme: Jesus becomes Emmanuel, "God with us," who has taken on our human qualities, becoming like us in all respects.

The assistant was tall. He was standing in the vestibule, greeting people as they walked out from Mass. Along came a little girl, hardly two feet tall, a human cherub if there ever was one. She looked up at the giant priest and said something he could not hear. He bent over, way down, as if he were going to touch his toes, and asked her to repeat what she said. In a piping voice, she asked: "What color are God's eyes?" Without a moment's hesitation the priest replied: "Blue, just like yours." Tiny as she was, the little girl was flattered. She blinked, smiled, and then toddled away to tell her mother.[5]

Application: Do we really believe that Jesus was human? What are the implications of this for us?

Holy Family

Luke 2:41–52

Finding Jesus in the Temple

Theme: In times of difficulty, families must focus on God's will for them.

Here is a child's legend about Jesus the Refugee. When Joseph and Mary were on their way to Egypt, the story runs, as the evening came they grew weary and sought refuge in a cave. It was very cold—so cold, in fact, that the ground was white with hoarfrost. A little spider saw the baby Jesus, and he wished so much that he could do something for him to keep him warm. He decided to do the only thing he could do—to spin his web across the entrance of the cave, to make a kind of curtain.

It happened that a detachment of Herod's soldiers came along that night, seeking children to kill to carry out Herod's blood-thirsty orders. When they came to the cave, they were about to burst in and search it when their captain noticed the spider's web. It was covered with the white hoarfrost and stretched right across the entrance of the cave.

He concluded that no one could possibly be in the cave, or they would have torn the spider's web. So the soldiers passed on and left the holy family in peace. And that, so they say, is why to this day we put tinsel on our Christmas trees; for the glittering tinsel streamers stand for the spider's web, white with hoarfrost, which kept the little refugee Christ-child safe in the cave on his way to Egypt.[6]

Application: What can we do as a family to recognize and honor Jesus?

The family had a very special guest coming for dinner, and the six-year-old son had been briefed to be on his very best behavior. As everyone sat down at the table, the boy reached for a roll and accidently knocked over his glass, spilling water all over the table. He froze in terror—he knew he was going to be scolded. The boy looked over at his father. His father looked at him, smiled, and knocked over his own water glass. Then, together, they got towels and wiped up the mess.[7]

Application: Do we identify with people when they make mistakes? Are we compassionate?

Solemnity of Mary

Luke 2:16–21

Mary Reflected on Daily Life with Jesus
Theme: In reflecting on "these things" in her heart, Mary grew in faith.

A story of two children. The parents of the first child were some-what mismatched. His father was unemployed with no formal schooling. His mother was a teacher. This child, born in Port

Huron, Michigan, was estimated to have an IQ of 81. He was withdrawn from school after three months—and was considered backward by school officials. The child enrolled in school two years late due to scarlet fever and respiratory infections. And he was going deaf. His emotional health was poor. He was stubborn, aloof, and showed very little emotion. He liked mechanics. He also liked to play with fire and burned down his father's barn. He showed some manual dexterity, but used very poor grammar. But he did want to be a scientist or a railroad mechanic.

The second child showed not much more promise either. This child was born of an alcoholic father. As a child she was sickly, bedridden, and often hospitalized. She was considered erratic and withdrawn. She would bite her nails and had numerous phobias. She wore a backbrace from a spinal defect and would constantly seek attention. She was a daydreamer with no vocational goals, although she expressed a desire to help the elderly and the poor.

Who were these children? The boy from Port Huron became one of the world's greatest inventors—Thomas A. Edison. And the awkward and sickly young girl became a champion of the oppressed—Eleanor Roosevelt. Would you have voted either one of these children "most likely to succeed?" Probably not.[8]

Theme: What norm do we use for judging a child's potential for good?

Epiphany

Matthew 2:1–12

Magi Journey to Jesus
Theme: Each person has to find Jesus in his or her own way.

As an old man was walking down the beach he noticed a young girl ahead of him picking up starfish and flinging them into the sea. He asked her why she was doing this. The little girl explained that a starfish stranded on the beach when the tide went out would die if left in the morning sun.

"But the beach goes on for miles and there are millions of starfish," said the old man. "How can your efforts make any difference?"

The little girl looked down the stretch of beach at all of the stranded starfish and then stared at the one in her hand. As she pitched it back into the salt water waves, she answered, "It makes a difference to this one."[9]

Application: Jesus values each person infinitely and each person can make a difference. Do we value the uniqueness of others?

Baptism of the Lord

Luke 3:15–16, 21–22

John Baptizes Jesus
Theme: Jesus' baptism and life make us a new creation.

California police and the courts have discovered the tattoos on teenagers are often more than a cosmetic decoration. A few years ago, a juvenile court judge in California observed that a large number of the teenagers appearing before him had tattoos— tattoos on the hands, fingers, and faces. The tattoos, he learned, identified the bearer as a member of some particular gang and, frequently, as a user of a particular drug. Many of these tattoos were self-inflicted by youths who were desperate to "belong." The judge also discovered that teenagers with visible tattoos were virtually excommunicated from the job market, since potential employers equated the tattoos with crimes and incompetency and refused to hire the youth.

The judge asked the Los Angeles County Medical Association if there might be, among its members, a plastic surgeon who, at no charge, would remove the tattoos from juvenile delinquents. Dr. Karl Stein, a well-known Los Angeles plastic surgeon, was the first to volunteer. Since 1981, Dr. Stein has turned around the lives of hundreds of his young patients through surgically removing the tattoos by excision, abrasion, laser, and virtually every other known method.[10]

Application: Your baptism is your tattoo, indelibly imprinted, identifying you as a disciple of Jesus. Would your neighbors see this in your daily life?

Lent

1st Sunday

Luke 4:1–13

Jesus Rebukes Satan with Scriptures
Theme: Jesus does not entertain Satan's temptations in the desert.

When Leonardo da Vinci was painting his masterpiece, "The Last Supper," he looked for a model for his Christ. At last, he located a chorister in one of the churches of Rome who was lovely in life and features, a young man named Pietro Bandinelli. Years passed, and the painting was unfinished. All the disciples had been painted save one—Judas Iscariot. Now da Vinci started to look for a man whose face was hardened and distorted by sin—and at last he found a beggar on the streets of Rome with a face so villainous that da Vinci shuddered when he looked at him. He hired the man to sit for him as he painted the face of Judas on his canvas. When he was about to dismiss the man, da Vinci said: "I have not yet found out your name." "I am Pietro Bandinelli. I also sat for you as your model of Christ."[11]

Application: How do we deal with temptation to sin, which can destroy the image of Christ in us?

2nd Sunday

Luke 9:28–36

The Transfiguration
Theme: Jesus gives us moments of light to prepare us for the darkness.

In her book, *Audacity to Believe*, Dr. Sheila Cassidy relates how she left England in 1971 to escape the "rat-race" professionalism of British medicine to go to Chile to work among the poorest of the poor. In 1975, Dr. Cassidy was arrested by the Chilean police for having treated the bullet wounds of a revolutionary leader. At an interrogation center she was stripped, tied to a bed, and tortured by electrodes attached to her body. Then she was placed in solitary confinement for three weeks and imprisoned in a detention camp for another five weeks before she was finally released and expelled from the country.

Dr. Cassidy writes: "I did not hate the men who had hurt us. . . . The freedom of spirit we enjoyed was something that our captors did not possess. Incredibly, in the midst of fear and loneliness I was filled with joy, for I knew without any vestige of doubt that God was with me, and that nothing they could do to me could change that."[12]

Application: Any transformation in us—transfiguration—has to come from within, by the power of God's grace. Do we pray for the Holy Spirit's guidance in this?

3rd Sunday
Luke 13:1–9

Call for Repentance
Theme: God, who is not mocked, expects good to come from creation.

We all get a second chance. Sometimes we blow it by thinking we can snow God, like the guy who was bothered by mice. He cut out a picture of a piece of cheese and put it in a mousetrap, thinking that mice were not too bright. The next day, when he visited his mousetrap, he found a picture of a mouse caught in a trap.[13]

Application: Like the fig tree in the parable, we are to bear good fruit. How are we preparing ourselves for this?

4th Sunday
Luke 15:1–3,11–32

The Prodigal Son
Theme: God always forgives.

In one of those ubiquitous Peanuts cartoon strips, Lucy is chasing Charlie Brown around and around the house. "I'll get you,

Charlie Brown, I'll get you!"

Suddenly Charlie Brown stops. Lucy comes to a screeching halt. Charlie Brown says: "If we, who are children, cannot forgive one another, how can we expect our parents, who are adult, to forgive one another, and in turn, how can the world . . ."

At this point Lucy punches Charlie Brown in the nose and knocks him down. Turning to a friend who has just come up, Lucy explains: "I had to hit him. He was beginning to make sense."[14]

Application: Do we really live a life of forgiveness?

5th Sunday
John 8:1–11

Woman Caught in Adultery
Theme: No one is worthy to cast the first stone.

A few years back a book entitled *I'm O.K., You're O.K.* was a best-seller. A priest gave a sermon using this theme from the book. After his sermon he asked a visiting priest waiting in the sacristy what he thought of his sermon. The visiting priest said, "I couldn't help imagining Jesus as he hung from the cross looking down and saying to his mother and to St. John: "If I'm O.K. and you're O.K., then what am I doing up here?"[15]

Application: We should judge no one because we are all in need of redemption. Have we judged anyone? Are we inclined to do this?

Passion (Palm) Sunday
Luke 22:14—23:56

The Passion
Theme: Jesus dies for the sins of humankind.

A soldier of the Argyll regiment [during World War II] was in a work detail on the railway. The day's work had ended; the tools were being counted, as usual. As the party was about to be dismissed, the Japanese guard shouted that a shovel was missing. He insisted that someone had stolen it to sell to the Thais. Striding up and down before the men, he ranted and denounced them for their wickedness and their ingratitude to the Emperor.

As he raved, he worked himself up into a paranoid fury. Screaming in broken English, he demanded that the guilty one step forward to take his punishment. No one moved; the guard's rage reached the heights of violence. "All die! All die!" he shrieked.

To show that he meant what he said, he cocked his rifle, put it on his shoulder and looked down the sights, ready to fire at the first man at the end of them. At that moment the Argyll stepped forward, stood stiffly to attention, and said calmly, "I did it."

The guard unleashed all his whipped-up hate; he kicked the helpless prisoner and beat him with his fists. Still the Argyll stood rigidly to attention, with the blood streaming down his face. His silence goaded the guard to excess rage. Seizing his rifle by the barrel, he lifted it high over his head and, with a final howl, brought it down on the skull of the Argyll, who sank limply to the ground and did not move. Although it was perfectly clear that he was dead, the guard continued to beat him and stopped only when he was exhausted.

The men of the work detail picked up their comrade's body, shouldered their tools and marched back to camp. When the tools were counted again at the guardhouse, no shovel was missing.[16]

Application: Even in small ways, we can live up to this: "No one has greater love than this, to lay down one's life for one's friends." In what ways can we "die for others"?

Easter

Easter Sunday
John 20:1–9

Jesus Raised from the Dead
Theme: As Jesus has risen, so will we who believe in him.

Ivan Turgenev, the author of *Fathers and Sons,* has written of an experience he had. One Easter he was in church. As he stood among many fair-haired Russian folk, a man came up and stood behind him. Turgenev sensed that the man was Christ. Then, overwhelmed by curiosity and awe, he looked at his neighbor. He saw ". . . a face like all men's faces." The Christ was an ordinary, ordinary man! That could not be! So the writer turned away. Then he knew that the peasant standing behind him was none other than Christ. He made another effort to control himself, but then he was haunted by the "same face" with its "everyday though unknown features." The novelist's heart sank, and he came to himself.

Only then did he realize ". . . that such a face . . . a face like all men's faces—is the face of Jesus." Only when we realize this will our love overcome our minds and we become true believers.[17]

Application: Can people see the joy of resurrection in our daily life?

2nd Sunday
John 20:19–31

Doubting Thomas
Theme: Doubt can be the seedbed of faith.

A rabbi and a soapmaker went for a walk together. The soapmaker said, "What good is religion? Look at all the trouble and misery of the world! Still there, even after years—thousands of years—of teaching about goodness and truth and peace. Still there, after all the prayers and sermons and teachings. If religion is good and true, why should this be?" The rabbi said nothing. They continued walking until he noticed a child playing in the gutter.

Then the rabbi said, "Look at that child. You say that soap makes people clean, but see the dirt on that youngster. Of what good is soap? With all the soap in the world, over all these years, the child is still filthy. I wonder how effective soap is, after all!"

The soapmaker protested, "But, Rabbi, soap cannot do any good unless it is used!"

"Exactly," replied the rabbi. "Exactly!"[18]

Application: When doubts of faith occur, we may actually be using our faith and this can be the occasion for stronger faith. "There lives more faith in honest doubt, believe me, than in half the creeds." (Alfred Lord Tennyson) Do we try to work through any doubts we may have about our faith?

3rd Sunday
John 21:1–19
Peter's Triple Confession of Love
Theme: Jesus always forgives us if we are sorry.

A couple of days after President Kennedy was tragically gunned down in Dallas, Texas, a Presbyterian church from the state of Michigan wrote to the wife of Lee Harvey Oswald. They had heard that she wished to stay in America and learn the English language. They took it upon themselves to write to her and invite her to come to their community with the promise of finding her a home that she might get a fresh start on a productive life. Unfortunately, many persons both in the local community and from around the nation got wind of this plan and began writing many critical letters about their offer to this widow.

One person probably described the situation most correctly when she said, "I never heard of a church doing anything like this before." She knew that forgiveness is not often found even in a group of believers who could probably best be called and known as "sinners anonymous." Forgiveness is so hard. The minister began the painstaking job of answering each letter that came across his desk that was both unkind and critical of the church's response. With great sensitivity he wrote each person a letter sharing that he understood their feelings and emotions about their efforts on behalf of Mrs. Oswald. However, he ended each letter by sharing, "The only thing you have not shown us is that what we have done would not have been done by our Lord and Savior Jesus Christ."[19]

Application: Right now, is there someone it would take a serious act of faith to forgive? Are you seriously willing to try?

4th Sunday
John 10:27–30

Jesus, the Good Shepherd
Theme: The voice of our shepherd, Jesus, leads us.

A string ensemble was rehearsing for their concert at a downtown church. The evening's program included a wonderful piece for the oboe. The oboist was exceptionally talented, but for some reason, the music sounded terrible.

The leader of the ensemble insisted that the oboe was out of tune, so the oboeist adjusted the reed of her instrument to bring it in tune with the other instruments. But the music continued to sound distorted and out of key. The other musicians were becoming increasingly critical and impatient. After several attempts, the leader proposed that the oboe part be dropped from the piece.

An elderly gentleman was sitting in the church during the ensemble's rehearsal. He quietly went up to the leader during a break in their practice and said, "Please forgive my intruding, but don't orchestras tune their instruments to the oboe?" The members of the ensemble were dumbfounded. They had overlooked a basic performance principle: an oboe sounds the proper pitch—it was the other instruments, tuned to one another, that were out of tune. When the other musicians tuned their instruments to the oboe, the music began to sound like music again.[20]

Application: Jesus always sets the note whereby we are to live. Do we have a spiritual director to help us recognize Jesus' voice?

5th Sunday

John 13:31–33, 34–35

Jesus Gives His Great Commandment of Love
Theme: We are to love each other as Jesus has loved us.

A story of love comes from 1976. A car accident tore open the head of a 21-year-old Chicago boy named Peter. His brain was damaged and he was thrown into a deep coma. Doctors told Peter's family and friends that he probably wouldn't survive. Even if he did, he'd always be in a comatose state.

In the sad days ahead, Peter's fiancée, Linda, spent all her spare time in the hospital. Night after night, she'd sit at Peter's bedside, pat his cheek, rub his brow, and talk to him. "It was like we were on a normal date," she said.

All the while Peter remained in a coma, unresponsive to Linda's loving presence. Night after night, for three and a half months, Linda sat at Peter's bedside, speaking words of encouragement to him, even though he gave no sign that he heard her.

Then one night Linda saw Peter's toe move. A few nights later she saw his eyelash flutter. This was all she needed. Against the advice of doctors, she quit her job and became his constant companion. She spent hours massaging his arms and legs.

Eventually she arranged to take him home. She spent all her savings on a swimming pool, hoping that the sun and the water would restore life to Peter's motionless limbs. Then came the day when Peter spoke his first word since the accident. It was only a grunt, but Linda understood it.

Gradually, with Linda's help, these grunts turned into words— clear words. Finally the day came when Peter was able to ask Linda's father if he could marry her. Linda's father said, "When you can walk down the aisle, Peter, she'll be yours."

Two years later Peter walked down the aisle of Our Lady of Pompeii Church in Chicago. He had to use a walker, but he was walking.

Every television station in Chicago covered that wedding. Newspapers across the country carried pictures of Linda and Peter. Celebrities phoned to congratulate them. People from as far away as Australia sent them letters. Families with loved ones in comas called to ask their advice.

Today, Peter is living a normal life. He talks slowly, but clearly. He walks slowly, but without a walker. He and Linda even have a lovely child.[21]

Application: Love and what it can accomplish is what every human life is all about. Are you open to loving others in a way comparable to the love in this story?

6th Sunday
John 14:23–29

Jesus Promises the Holy Spirit of Peace
*Theme: The peace Jesus promises us will come to us
from the Father by means of the Holy Spirit.*

Amid the horror of World War I, there occurred a unique truce when, for a few hours, enemies were brothers and songs of peace replaced artillery shells. By Christmas 1914, the war was only five months old and already more than 800,000 soldiers had been killed or wounded. Christmas Day itself was expected to be just another bloody day of the bloody war—but something strange happened.

A British Tommy on guard heard a strangely familiar sound drifting across the narrow strip of no-man's-land between the trenches. A lone German voice was singing *"Stille Nacht, heilige Nacht. . . ."*

The British sentry began to sing the English words to the melody, "Silent Night, Holy Night." A comrade crawled up to the sentry station and joined in. Little by little, others on both sides picked up the melody.

The Germans soon began a second carol, *"O Tannenbaum,"* and the British replied with "God Rest Ye Merry, Gentlemen." On and on the antiphonal singing went. Soon signs appeared on both sides, scrawled in two languages: "Merry Christmas."

One by one soldiers started laying down their arms and crept beneath the barbed wire and around mortar holes into no-man's-land, until scores of British and German troops met together in the first light of Christmas Day. Photographs of mothers and wives were brought out, gifts of candy and cigarettes were exchanged. Even a soccer ball was produced—the British beat the Germans, 3 to 2.

By mid-morning, horrified officers summoned their men back. The soldiers obeyed and the grisly business of war resumed. But for a few hours their master was neither King nor Kaiser, but the Prince of Peace.[22]

Application: In what ways do we, who have been given the Spirit, work for the peace that Jesus wills for us?

7th Sunday
John 17:20–26

Jesus Prays for Unity
Theme: The love of God unites us with God and with one another.

In Yakima, Washington, sometime back, a dying man made a strange request. On his deathbed, Grant Flory said to his family: "Get me to the Mustangs' playoffs. No matter what." He was referring to his old high school team, the Prosser Mustangs. So in early December, when the Mustangs played in Seattle's Kingdome, Flory's cremated remains were in attendance. His son Dwight approached the stadium gate wearing a camera bag that contained his father's urn. He was stopped by a guard who asked what was in the bag.

"It's my dad," he replied. The guard looked puzzled but allowed the ashes inside. Family members said anyone who knew Grant Flory wouldn't be surprised by his request. He was a real football fan.[23]

Application: How dedicated and concerned are we to be united with God in prayer at least once a day?

Pentecost

John 20:19–23

The Holy Spirit Descends on the Apostles
Theme: We, too, are filled with the Holy Spirit.

A little girl was visiting her grandmother in a small country town in the South. They attended a very emotional religious service, where people expressed their feelings by jumping about and shouting . . . what we might call a "Holy Roller" service.

The little girl asked her grandmother if all the jumping meant the Holy Spirit was really there. Her grandmother said, "Honey, it don't matter how high they jump up, it's what they do when they come down that will tell you if it is the real thing."[24]

Application: It would be good if we were a little more enthusiastic about our religion, but what matters is what we do in everyday life. Does the Holy Spirit have a practical effect on our daily life? In what way?

Trinity Sunday

John 16:12–15

The Spirit of Truth
Theme: Jesus continues to send us the Spirit of truth.

A priest was sitting in a Chicago airport waiting for his plane. A man sat down beside him and began to give his opinions on religion. He boasted: "I won't accept anything I can't understand. Take this business of three Gods in one God or whatever it is. I can't buy that. Nobody can explain it to me, so I will not believe it."

Pointing to the sun streaming in the window, the priest asked: "Do you believe in the sun?" "Why, of course," the doubter admitted. "All right," the priest continued, "the rays you see coming through that window are from the sun, 90,000,000 miles from here. The heat we feel comes from both the sun and from its rays. The Holy Trinity is something like that. The sun is God the Father; the sun sends out its rays, God the Son. Then from both the sun and its rays, from the Father and the Son, proceeds or comes the Holy Spirit, the heat. Can you explain how that happens?" The doubter quickly changed the subject.[25]

Application: There is more to life than meets the eye. Do we pray that the Holy Spirit may sharpen our vision so that we may see things as God sees them?

Corpus Christi
Luke 9:11–17
Miracle of Loaves and Fishes
Theme: Jesus feeds us with his body and blood.

Shortly after undergoing major surgery, a woman decided to put her thoughts in writing. She wrote: "When someone said that when Jesus referred to the Passover wine as his blood, and then shared it with his disciples, he was being cannibalistic, I could not help thinking of the modern practice of giving blood by transfusion. While it isn't eaten, the blood is definitely taken into the body in a life-giving way.

"After surgery I had a vivid experience of this type of life-receiving from a blood transfusion. All day, in the recovery room, my only conscious feeling was the awful coldness, in the middle of summer. Nothing seemed to bring warmth to my body. I was inert and completely uninterested in anything going on around me.

"I finally was aware of a timing of two hours which seemed to be the time taken for the careful dripping of this blood into my veins. Suddenly, I felt warmth pour over me right out to my fingertips and to the ends of my toes. I seemed to come up from the bottom of the sea. I felt like smiling and greeting someone.

"I opened my eyes. The first thing I did was to find a clock. This seemed to relate me to my own real world. I was amazed that it was nearly midnight and I was elated to think I was alive and warm and happy.

"Then I saw the doctor and I couldn't help joking with him about keeping such awful hours. I heard him say, 'Now you can go home,' so everything was all right.

"Later, I felt I would give anything I own—anything—to find the stranger whose blood had brought this warmth, this life to me. Now I walk the streets, grateful to some unknown person whose very blood flows in my veins and contributes to my daily joy. This is a debt I can never repay."[26]

Application: We are united in a faith community around the life-bringing Eucharist. Do we feel the need for, or the effect of, being nourished by the Eucharist?

Ordinary Time

2nd Sunday

John 2:1–12

Wedding at Cana

Theme: By his presence at the wedding,
Jesus sanctified and endorsed the sacredness of marriage.

In a recent Sunday Doonesbury comic strip, Mike Doonesbury clicked on his television set and flipped to one of those daytime tabloid talk shows that are long on sensationalism and short on reality. The host began the program: "Meet Brad and Carol. Brad and Carol have been married for ten years. They have two happy, well-adjusted children who were not born out of wedlock. Both Brad and Carol go to church, give time to charities, love their parents, and help their kids with their homework. Neither has ever battered the other. Neither is addicted to sex, drugs, alcohol, food, violence, cigarettes, or each other. Today on Geraldo: Happily married people who are not recovering from *anything*!

"So, Brad and Carol! What's it like being freaks?"

"It's fine. No complaints."

"Actually, it's strengthened our marriage."[27]

Application: The Christian view of marriage is opposed to the world's. Do we have the courage to witness the Christian view of marriage?

3rd Sunday

Luke 1:1–4; 4:14–21

Jesus Preaches in Galilee

Theme: Jesus announces that the Spirit of the Lord is upon him.

Although born without a right hand, Jim Abbott became a star pitcher at the University of Michigan, the ace of the U.S. teams in

---

the 1987 Pan Am Games and the 1988 Olympics, and last season, despite pitching for a last-place team, was one of the best pitchers in the American league . . . even though he has only one hand. He answers 300 pieces of mail a week, personally responding to those who need encouragement or reassurance. And he always makes time in every city for kids. "Did kids ever tease you?" a curly-haired youngster name Kevin—also with only one hand—once asked Abbott. "Yeah, they did," and Abbott told the youngster how kids used to laugh and say his hand looked like a foot. The little boy said that they call him "Crab."

Abbott then asked the boy if he thought his hand is a problem. No, the boy replied. Then Abbott asked, "Is there anything you can't do?" "No," the boy said. And Abbott told his young friend, "Well, I don't think [it's a problem] either. . . . Look at me. I'm playing with these guys. There's Dave Winfield and Dave Parker and Wally Joyner. I'm playing with them and I'm just like you."[28]

Application: With faith in Jesus, we can do wonderful things for the Kingdom of God. Do we really believe this? In what ways can we show it?

4th Sunday

Luke 4:21–30

Jesus Rejected in His Hometown
Theme: Proclaiming the Word of God can be very risky.

Alfred W. Hurst tells about a minister who sent a New Testament to be rebound. When it came back, he was surprised to find it labeled in gilt letters, T.N.T. There was no room to spell out "The New Testament," so the bookbinder had inscribed merely the first letters of the three words, T.N.T. Quite frankly, that's not a bad name for the New Testament. On the day of Pentecost it is reported that suddenly there came from heaven a sound of the rising of a mighty wind. Moffatt translates it "a mighty blast."[29]

Application: The committed Christian, like Jesus, will be persecuted. What risks are we honestly willing to take for Jesus?

5th Sunday

Luke 5:1–11

Jesus Calls Simon Peter

Theme: Jesus calls us to follow him.

Today's gospel might become more striking if we imagined its author, Luke, alive today and talking with a Hollywood agent about coming out with a book.

I imagine a producer named Sid, lunching at some spectacular trendy Beverly Hills watering hole with a young writer named Luke. Between cellular phone calls and name-dropping, Sid tells Luke, "Bob's agent sent me your fisherman property. Loved it, Luke. It's so . . . rustic, so universal, so nostalgic for a bygone era. It's gonna need a rewrite, though."

"What's wrong with it, Sid?" says Luke.

"Now, don't get nervous," replies Sid between bites of arugula and endive salad. "I told you I loved it. The Peter character is too weak, though. He's got to be more of a hero. What star is going to take a role like that?"

Luke asks, "What did you have in mind?"

"Everything is fine until he says, 'Leave me, Lord. I am a sinful man.' I see Peter as more of an entrepreneur. Why can't he say, 'Hey, Jesus, that was fantastic! I think you and I can go places. With our boats and your fishing radar, we could make a killing!' "And the ending isn't right, either. What happens to all those fish? It says the fishermen leave everything behind. Not very practical, Luke-babe, not to mention environmental concerns. I see it as a partnership. Peter bankrolls his preacher-friend with the money he makes off the catch. Why not God and Mammon? What were you trying to get across with that 'catching human beings' line, anyway?"[30]

Application: Are we alert and primed to hear God's call to us in our particular circumstances?

6th Sunday

Luke 6:17, 20–26

Sermon on the Plain

Theme: Jesus calls blessed those poor who have faith.

A remarkable Hasidic rabbi, Levi Yitzhak of Berdichev in the Ukraine, used to say that he had discovered the meaning of love from a drunken peasant. The rabbi was visiting the owner of a tavern in the Polish countryside. As he walked in, he saw two peasants at a table. Both were gloriously in their cups. Arms around each other, they were protesting how much each loved the other. Suddenly Ivan said to Peter: "Peter, tell me, what hurts me?" Bleary-eyed, Peter looked at Ivan: "How do I know what hurts you?" Ivan's answer was swift: "If you don't know what hurts me, how can you say you love me?"[31]

Application: Jesus knows our hurts and needs, expressed in the beatitudes, and loves us. Do we really believe that the poor in spirit and the mourning are blessed?

7th Sunday

Luke 6:27–38

Love Your Enemies

*Theme: Jesus tells us we are to love our enemies
and turn the other cheek.*

We have examples of the forgiveness Jesus is speaking of in today's gospel. In his *Les Miserables*, Victor Hugo shows an ex-convict, Jean Valjean, just released from nineteen years in the galleys for the crime of stealing bread to feed his sister's children. No one, upon his release, will sell him food or shelter because of his criminal record. Hopeless and exhausted, he stumbles into the house of a saintly bishop, who greets him courteously as an honored guest and offers him the best hospitality at his disposal.

Valjean, bewildered by the bishop's kindness and desperate to survive, flees in the middle of the night, taking with him the silver plates from the bishop's table. In the morning, the bishop is troubled not by the abuse of hospitality, not by the treachery and theft, but by his own want of charity. "I have for a long time wrongfully withheld this silver; it belonged to the poor. Who was this man? A poor man evidently," he reasons to himself.

When the police arrive with the captured Valjean, the bishop's silver in his possession, the bishop calmly greets the thief and says, "But I gave you the candlesticks also, which are silver like the rest. . . .Why did you not take them along with the plates?" The police reluctantly release Valjean, since the bishop insists that no theft has occurred, and Valjean "stands confounded" before the bishop. The bishop hands Valjean the candlesticks and pronounces a blessing: "Jean Valjean, my brother: You belong no longer to evil, but to good. It is your soul that I am buying for you. I withdraw it from dark thoughts and . . . I give it to God."

Valjean meant his theft for evil, but God and the bishop meant it for good. And the good that comes of that transforming mercy is largely what the rest of the book is about.[32]

Application: Are Jesus' sayings about forgiveness and love realistic?

8th Sunday
Luke 6:39–45

Good Tree, Good Fruit
Theme: The pure of heart bring forth works of justice.

In the Middle Ages a man was refining gold in a fire-heated pot on a street corner. A little child asked him what he was doing. He said he was removing the impurities that rose to the top as the ore melted. "How will you know when you're done?" the child asked. "When I can see my face perfectly reflected in the gold," the man said.[33]

Application: God purifies our hearts and words so that in looking at them, God can see reflected back the image of the Son. How do we view the role of suffering in our life?

9th Sunday

Luke 7:1–10

Jesus Heals Official's Servant
Theme: Faith is needed for healing.

Bruce Larson tells a story in his book, *Edge of Adventure*. It's about a letter found in a baking powder tin wired to the handle of an old pump, which offered the only hope of drinking water on a very long and seldom used trail across the Armagosa Desert in the USA; the letter read as follows:

"This pump is all right as of June 1932. I put the new leather sucker washer into it, and it ought to last several years. But this leather washer dries out and the pump has got to be primed. Under the white rock, I buried a bottle of water. There's enough water in it to prime the pump, but not if you drink some first. Pour in about one-quarter, and let her soak to wet the leather. Then pour in the rest, medium fast, and pump like crazy. You'll get water. The well has never run dry. Have faith. When you get watered up, fill the bottle and put it back like you found it for the next feller." (Signed) Desert Pete.

"P.S. Don't go drinking up the water first. Prime the pump with it first, and you'll get all you can hold."[34]

Application: Is our desire to be healed based on deep faith in God's loving concern for us?

10th Sunday

Luke 7:11-17

Jesus Heals Widow's Son
Theme: We must be compassionate as Jesus is.

At a retreat for peace, conducted in Los Angeles by Thich Nhat Hahn, a Vietnamese monk, some American veterans of the War were invited to attend, and to share their stories. With tears of shame and regret one veteran confessed how before combat he and his buddies would throw money into a jar and whoever killed the most enemies that day would get the money.

Another veteran told how one day during the war he captured a young Vietnamese soldier. With his hands clasped on his head, the Vietnamese soldier captive fell down on his knees and crawled. Moved by the look of absolute terror in his enemy's eyes, the American soldier began to ask him questions through an interpreter.

"How old are you?"

"Nineteen."

"So am I. What do you do?"

"I'm a student."

"So am I. Do you have a girlfriend?"

"Yes."

"So do I."

Then, reaching into his knapsack, the young American pulled out a tin of beans, gave it to his enemy and let him go. At first the Vietnamese ran as fast as he could, zigzagging back and forth for fear that he would be shot in the back. Then suddenly he turned, raised the tin of beans high over his head, bowed a deep bow and disappeared into the jungle. For this Vietnamese soldier a tin of beans was a feast to be shared. From that day on the young American soldier marched with his gun turned upside down.[35]

Application: Every day there may be opportunities to show compassion in action. Do we look for them?

11th Sunday

Luke 7:36—8:3

A Woman Wipes Jesus' Feet
Theme: Love and forgiveness are closely connected.

An old man once saw a scorpion that had become tangled in the roots of an old tree in a swamp. The old man crawled out on the tree's gnarled roots and tried to help the scorpion free itself. But each time he did, the scorpion bit him. On shore a smart-alecky kid laughed at the old man. "Hey, old man, all you're getting out of trying to help that scorpion is a swollen hand. What a fool you are."

The old man replied simply. "Just because it is the scorpion's nature to sting, should I change mine, which is to save?"[36]

Application: Are we willing to help people, including forgiving them, even at risk to ourselves?

12th Sunday

Luke 9:18–24

Jesus Predicts His Passion
Theme: We can follow Jesus only by dying to ourselves.

Robert was born at Aldershot; his mother was Japanese and father English. When Robert started school, he was tormented by the other children. One Christmas, his parents bought him a watch, but this was taken from him by some other older children and thrown against the school wall. The school crossing warden asked Robert one day why he was walking over a mile to school and crossing a busy road instead of using the school bus. His parents had wanted him to use the bus but Robert had refused. He told the traffic warden he was frightened of the other children because they called him a "wog," a "Chink," and a "bloody Jap"! He also said that Jesus had told us to love our enemies. He walked to school for three weeks. One day, when crossing the road he was knocked down by a car and killed.[37]

Application: Living as Jesus' disciples will require sacrifice of us. Do we put a limit on what we would be willing to undergo?

13th Sunday

Luke 9:51–62

Discipleship
Theme: Jesus calls us to follow him in commitment.

Gary, a farmer, is concerned that the insecticides he uses are killing birds and beneficial insects and polluting the air. But he says that switching to a safer, but more expensive, pest control system would endanger his profit margin and his family's financial security.

Kristen cries whenever she sees evidence of cruelty to or exploitation of animals. She refuses to eat meat and sends large donations to animal rights groups. Yet when her husband buys her a fur-trimmed coat, she wears it rather than risk hurting his feelings.

Richie joins in his Boy Scout troop's project to devise a recycling plan for use in each scout's home. After a few weeks, though, he goes back to dumping all his family's trash into big plastic bags for the trash collector. He says he didn't realize that sorting and saving would cut so much into the time he needed for soccer practice.[38]

Application: Is our discipleship a half-heartedness or lukewarm commitment?

14th Sunday

Luke 10:1–12,17–20

Jesus Instructs His Disciples on Mission
Theme: We all have the vocation to witness to Jesus in our society.

In the early 1980s, we heard a lot about the "dirty war" in Argentina. A military junta had taken over the government. They secretly killed many of their enemies without trial. Opposing this totalitarian terror required heroism.

The heroism we heard most about was the heroism of the mothers. Without formal organization, a group of mothers began assembling in the square outside the presidential palace at a certain time on a certain day each week. They were the women whose adult children were among the missing. They met without formality and without speeches, but they met weekly, and walked quietly around the square.

They wore white scarfs and each carried a photo and the name of her missing child. It was a strange scene: unarmed, unimportant women, wearing white, walking quietly, silently insisting. You can guess that it required courage, but you could hardly guess at the power and importance of what they did.

Their simple protest had an enormous impact on local public awareness and on worldwide opinion. Their simple, determined protest contributed to the return of civilian government and then eventually to the arrest and trial of the military responsible for the reign of terror.

The mothers in white did not have the voice of power but they exercised the voice of the poor. They did not have the authority of power but they exercised the power of authority.[39]

Application: To what extent do we mirror in society Jesus' power of authority?

15th Sunday

Luke 10:25–37

Good Samaritan

Theme: Our commitment is seen in our dying to self to help another.

M. Scott Peck begins his book, *The Different Drummer*, with a powerful story. An old abbot of a dying community of monks goes into the woods to seek the advice of a neighboring town's rabbi. The abbot is hoping that the rabbi can give him some pearls of wisdom that might save the order from dying out. However, the old monk comes back to the monastery very discouraged. "He cannot help," the abbot tells the few monks left. "The only thing he did say just as I was leaving—it was something very cryptic— was that the Messiah is one of us. I don't know what he meant."

Despite the fact that they did not understand, not one of the monks could forget the rabbi's words. And they thought about their meaning. Me? The Messiah? No way. I could never be that important to God. One of my brothers? The Messiah? I know these men—they are not perfect by any means. And then, something happened.

As Peck explains, "The old monks began to treat each other with extraordinary respect. Then it happened that some of the younger men who came to visit the monastery started to talk more and more with the old monks. After a while, one asked if he could join them. Then another. And another. Within a few years, the monastery was filled again with monks."[40]

Application: Do we treat others as we would Jesus?

16th Sunday
Luke 10:38–42

Martha and Mary
Theme: Discipleship takes many forms.

There was once a man who was trying to read the evening newspaper after he had come home from a rough day at the office. As he attempted to read the paper, he was constantly being interrupted by his children. One child came and asked for money for an ice cream cone, and his father gently reached into his pocket and gave him the necessary coin. Another child arrived in tears. Her leg was hurt and she wanted her daddy to kiss the hurt away. An older son came with an algebra problem, and they eventually arrived at the right answer. Finally, the last and youngest of them all burst into the room looking for good old dad. The father said cynically, "What do you want?" The little youngster said, "Oh, Daddy, I don't want anything. I just want to sit in your lap."[41]

Application: Is being present to another a form of service or ministry?

> Christ came into my room and stood there
> and I was bored to death.
> I had work to do.
> I wouldn't have minded if he'd been crippled or something
> —I do well with cripples—
> but he just stood there, all face
> and with that damned guitar.
> I didn't ask him to sit down;
> He'd have stayed all day.
> Let's be honest. You can be crucified just so often—
> then you've had it.
> I mean you're useless; no good to God,

let alone to anybody else.
So I said to him after a while,
Well, what's up? What do you want?
And he laughed, stupid,
said he was just passing by
and thought he'd say hello.
Great, I said. Hello.
So he left.
And I was so damned mad
I couldn't even listen to the radio. I went
and got some coffee.
The trouble with Christ is
he always comes at the wrong time.[42]

Application: We meet Jesus in those around us, and it isn't always convenient. Do we try to have Jesus, in the person of others, come to us only when it is convenient?

17th Sunday
Luke 11:1–13

The Our Father
Theme: We should pray as Jesus prayed, to our Father.

The daughter of Karl Marx once confessed to a friend that she had never been brought up in any religion and had never been religious. "But," she said, "the other day I came across a beautiful prayer which I very much wish could be true." "And what was that prayer?" she was asked. Slowly the daughter of Karl Marx began repeating in German, "Our Father, who art in heaven . . ."[43]

Application: Do we understand God as "our Father" merely as a metaphor or as reality? Do we pray the Our Father daily?

18th Sunday

Luke 12:13–21

Jesus Warns About Greed

Theme: One's life does not consist in the abundance of possessions.

There is a story told of an English nobleman of tremendous wealth who gave his jester a wand, saying, "Keep this wand until you find a greater fool than yourself." The jester laughingly accepted the wand and used it on festive occasions. One day, the nobleman lay dying. Calling the jester to his bedside, he said, "I am going on a long journey." "Where to?" asked the jester. "I don't know," came the reply. "What provisions have you made for the trip?" the jester asked. The nobleman shrugged his shoulders. "None at all." "Then," said the jester, "take this." And placing the wand in the nobleman's hands, he added, "It belongs to you. You are a greater fool than I."[44]

Application: We are to concentrate not on riches, but on our union with God and one another. Do we see greed as the root cause of evil in society? As a component of capitalism?

19th Sunday

Luke 12:32–48

The Master's Return

Theme: We are to be ready for Jesus' return.

A missionary priest from Europe was stationed in Hong Kong. When he heard that a famous missionary had died in south China, he made a pilgrimage to that village. Dressed in shorts and a sport shirt, he met two elderly women on the road. As he passed he said, "Good day." "You are Catholic," one woman stated.

The priest was startled and she went on to explain that the only foreigners who speak Chinese are priests. He accompanied them to their village, which was entirely Catholic. When he inquired how long since a priest had visited them, they replied, "In 1951."

They did not know any prayers in Chinese, but prayed and sang with the priest in Latin. Later, when he was leaving the village, the priest saw the woman who had first spoken to him. She was dancing and shouting,

"Today, God has blessed me."[45]

Application: Faith is a gift; once given, we must cultivate it and pass it on. What intensity of faith are we passing on to our descendants?

20th Sunday

Luke 12:49–53

Jesus Has Come to Light a Fire on Earth
Theme: Jesus' fire is to spread over Earth.

The fourth graders were studying the Pilgrims coming to America and settling in New England. The teacher asked, "Why did the Puritans leave England for America?" A pupil immediately raised his hand and answered: "So that they could carry on their religion in freedom in their own way, and force others to do the same."[46]

Application: Is our faith a fire burning within? Would others know we are Christian by observing us day to day?

21st Sunday

Luke 13:22–30

The Kingdom of God
Theme: We enter heaven through a narrow gate, not a broad pathway.

There's a legendary fisherman down in Louisiana who catches lots of fish. One day a stranger came to his cabin on the bayou and asked him if he would take him fishing. As they got into the boat, the stranger noticed the famous fisherman had no rod or reel—just an old rusty tackle box and a net.

After a while, they came into an isolated cove surrounded by tall, massive oaks draped with Spanish moss. The stranger watched with interest as the fisherman reached down into the tackle box, pulled out a stick of dynamite, lit the fuse, and threw it into the water.

There was a muffled explosion followed by the surfacing of a number of dead fish, which the fisherman proceeded to scoop up with his net. Whereupon the stranger pulled out a big badge and announced, "I caught you. I'm the game warden. You know it's illegal to blow up fish!"

The notorious fisherman didn't bat an eye. He calmly reached down into his tackle box, pulled out another stick of dynamite, lit the fuse, and handed it to the game warden. "Well," he asked the stunned warden, "are you gonna fish or you gonna just sit there?"[47]

Application: Would Jesus say to us, "You just gonna sit there?" Would he recognize us as working to establish the Kingdom of God?

22nd Sunday

Luke 14:1,7–14

Humbling Oneself
Theme: We are to humbly serve the needs of others.

An ancient teacher once asked his pupils how to tell when the night had ended and the day was on the way back. "Could it be," asked one student, "when you can see an animal in the distance and can tell whether it is a sheep or a dog?"

"No," said the teacher.

"Could it be," asked another, "when you can look at a tree and tell whether it is a fig tree or a peach tree?"

"No," answered the teacher.

"Well, then when is it?" demanded his pupils.

"It is when you look on the face of any woman or any man and see that she or he is your sister or brother. Because if you cannot do this, no matter what time it is, it is still night."[48]

Application: Loving others in act on a daily basis is what lights up the world. Do we put ourselves at the service of others? How?

23rd Sunday

Luke 14:25–33

Need for Prudent Commitment

Theme: We must be aware of the cost Jesus requires of us as disciples.

A frog found himself trapped on a large lily pad surrounded by hungry alligators. His only hope for escape was to hop over the alligators to the next lily pad. An owl, sitting on a branch over-head, said with cool detachment: "Why don't you just take off and fly? Just fly to the next pad."

The frog got a running start, flapped his legs as fast and as hard as he could, lifted off, and came down right in front of the massive jaws of a giant reptile.

"Stupid owl!" the frog screamed. "Frogs can't fly."

"Please," said the owl disdainfully, "that's an implementation issue. I only deal in concepts."[49]

Application: We should consider what being a disciple really means, make a firm commitment, and then put it into action. Are we courageous enough to do this?

24th Sunday

Luke 15:1–32

The Prodigal Son

Theme: The Father never stops loving us.

In one of the episodes of the comic strip "Peanuts," Lucy has a he-lium-filled balloon which she gives to Snoopy, saying, "I'm going in for lunch, Snoopy. . . . Hold this for me."

She puts the string of the balloon in his mouth and warns him, "Whatever you do, don't let go of it!"

So Snoopy sits there motionless, holding the balloon. It must have been a long lunch, because eventually he falls asleep, still holding on to the balloon. During his nap he yawns and, of course, the balloon takes off.

In that twilight zone between sleeping and waking he realizes what just happened and is suddenly wide awake in a panic. In the final frame he is walking along a railroad track in the moonlight, with his belongings in a sack tied to a pole on his shoulder, saying to himself, "Make one mistake and you're doomed for life!"[50]

Application: Unlike Snoopy, we should not feel we are doomed for life. Forgiveness, a second chance, can always be ours. Are we prepared to give others a second chance?

25th Sunday
Luke 16:1–13

Parable of the Unjust Steward
*Theme: Jesus wants us to be as clever as serpents
and as simple as doves.*

Dr. Mimi Silbert, criminologist and psychologist, helped found the successful Delancy Street Foundation for ex-convicts 21 years ago. The late Dr. Karl Menninger described it as "the best and most successful rehabilitation program I have studied in the world." Every participant leaves with a high school equivalency diploma and learns three skills which prepare them for the work force. Dr. Silbert began by renting a home and volunteering the residents for any physical work the neighbors might need.

Today these ex-cons operate a moving company, a fine restaurant, and a retail complex. All this is done without grants or professional staff. The program is strictly a self-help venture with each participant involved both as a student and a teacher. This pooling of skills and resources has helped graduate thousands of men and women into society "as taxpaying citizens leading successful lives."[51]

Application: Do we use money to further the kingdom of God? Do we try to see the good in people, their potential?

26th Sunday

Luke 16:19–31

Dives and Lazarus

Theme: The rich have grave responsibilities to the needy.

There is a Jewish story about Rabbi Joshua, the son of Levi, and a trip to Rome in the third century. He was astounded to behold the magnificence of the buildings. He was especially struck by the care lavished upon statues, which were covered with exquisite cloth to protect them from the summer heat. As he was admiring the beauty of Roman art, a beggar plucked at his sleeve and asked for a crust of bread. The sage looked at the statues and turning to the man in rags, he said, "Here are statues of stone covered with expensive clothes. Here is a man, created in the image of God, covered with rags. A civilization that pays more attention to statues than to human beings shall surely perish."[52]

Application: What are our statues, our priorities? The poor and powerless, the illiterate, the homeless, the ill?

27th Sunday

Luke 17:5–10

Faith Moving Mountains

Theme: Faith leads to duty well done.

Paganini, the great violinist, came out before his audience one day and made the discovery just as the applause ended that there was something wrong with his violin. He looked at it a second and then saw that it was not his famous and valuable one. He felt paralyzed for a moment, then turned to his audience and told them there had been some mistake and he did not have his own violin. He stepped back behind the curtain thinking that it was still where he had left it, but discovered that someone had stolen his and left that old secondhand one in its place. He remained back of the curtain a moment, then came out before his audience and said: "Ladies and gentlemen, I will show you that the music is not in the instrument but in the soul." And he played as he had never played before; and out of that secondhand instrument, the music poured forth until his audience was enraptured with enthusiasm and the applause almost lifted the roof off the building, because the man had revealed to them that the music was not in the machine but in his own soul.[53]

Application: Is your faith deep in your heart and not only something external? Do we seek ways to express our faith in action?

28th Sunday

Luke 17:11–19

Ten Lepers

Theme: Giving thanks to God nourishes our soul, makes us joyful.

Winston Churchill loved to tell the story of the little boy who fell off a pier into deep ocean water. An older sailor, heedless of the great danger to himself, dove into the stormy water, struggled with the boy, and finally, exhausted, brought him to safety. Two days later the boy's mother came with him to the same pier, seeking the sailor who rescued her son. Finding him, she asked, "You dove into the ocean to bring my boy out?"

"I did," he replied.

The mother quickly demanded, "Then where's his hat?"[54]

Application: When we do what we believe is right, we shouldn't always expect gratitude. How often do we thank God for all that we have been given?

29th Sunday

Luke 18:1–8

Widow Pesters Judge for Justice

Theme: God expects us to persevere in prayer.

St. Bernard was riding on his horse one day, lost in prayer. He met a beggar on the road and engaged in conversation with him.

The beggar asked Bernard what he was doing on the horse as he went along, and Bernard said he was praying.

"But I often have distractions in my prayer," Bernard confessed.

"Oh, well, I never have distractions when I pray," the beggar said.

"That's nice," said St. Bernard. "I'll give you this horse if you can say an 'Our Father' without once being distracted."

"Oh, that's easy," the beggar said, and he began to pray, "Our Father, who art in heaven; hallowed be thy name . . ." The beggar paused. "Say, does the saddle come with the horse?"[55]

Application: When we pray, we should not lose heart if we are distracted or if the prayer seems dry. Do we persevere in prayer?

30th Sunday
Luke 18:9–14

Pharisee and Publican
Theme: Self-righteousness is not of God.

One sunny day an elephant was taking a dip in a jungle pool. A mouse came to the edge of the pond and demanded that the elephant come out. "Why?" asked the elephant. "I'll tell you why when you get out," said the mouse. So the elephant got out and asked, "OK. What do you want?" The mouse replied, "I just wanted to see if you were wearing my bathing suit."[56]

Application: In what ways do we exaggerate our importance and consider ourselves superior to others?

31st Sunday
Luke 19:1–10

Zacchaeus Climbs a Tree
Theme: Jesus seeks out everyone.

A little girl heard her minister read from Luke's gospel the words spoken concerning Jesus by the religious Pharisees: "This man receives sinners and eats with them." She pricked up her ears and after the service was over she went up to the minister and said, "I didn't know my name was in the Bible." The pastor said, "Why, Edith, I don't believe it is." "Oh, yes, you read it this morning. The part that said Jesus receives sinners and Edith with them."[57]

Application: Are we convinced that we are important in God's eyes? Does this conviction change the way we live?

32nd Sunday

Luke 20:27–38

Pharisees Try to Trick Jesus About Divorce
Theme: God's word is a living word.

This story happened last summer. A friend of mine had gone to a Gay Pride march in a midwestern city. . . .After the march, several gay and lesbian people gathered in an auditorium for worship. At the front of the room the minister of the Metropolitan Community Church was trying to begin the service. He could hardly be heard over a jeering group of protestors at the back of the hall. They had come from another Christian church in the city.

"Sinners!" they shouted, "Repent of your sick and evil ways!" The protestors got louder and angrier, waving their Bibles over their heads. The young minister invited the gay and lesbian people to move forward. Then, the whole group at the front turned to face those at the back. "Shame. Shame. Shame," they chanted softly, shaking their heads. Then their chanting changed; taking their cue from the minister they began to say: "Jesus loves me and Jesus loves you. Jesus loves me and Jesus loves you." Over and over, the gay group to the protestors.

But that was too much. Suddenly, one, then another, and soon another of the protestors jumped up on tables at the back of the room. Soon, they were all screaming together, "Jesus hates you! Jesus hates you! Jesus hates you!" The words came with such violent anger that many of the gay people grew silent, fearing for their lives. My friend was afraid, too.

But more than that, she was filled with rage and sorrow. Sorrow that the name of Jesus could be so violently taken in vain. What would ever give anyone the right to say, "Jesus hates you," to another human being? What sort of faith is this? What witness so righteous, so right, that Jesus' name could ever be used for such hateful condemnation?

I wish I could tell you that I made up this story. I did not. Indeed I fear it has probably been repeated many times, in many places.[58]

Application: People often twist Jesus' words to their own purpose and make them mean what they want them to mean. Do we do this?

33rd Sunday
Luke 21:5–19

Jesus Describes End Times
Theme: The end times will not be as we expect them.

Tom Riley was a devoted grandfather, ready volunteer, and good friend. He loved life.

Problem. At some point many years ago he had come to the conclusion that he would die before his sixty-eighth birthday. When he first began talking about it, his family found it amusing.

Then he started to act on the belief in earnest a couple of years before he was to turn sixty-eight. He made sure his will was in order. He visited the Grand Canyon, a longtime dream. He gave away his golf clubs. Despite a doctor's clean bill of health, he took to his bed.

Then something happened: a month before that fateful birthday, his eldest grandson, his favorite, was hit by a car while riding a bicycle. His family visited the boy, leaving Tom home. Imagine their surprise when he walked into the hospital. He had driven there, even though he had let his driver's license lapse six months ago.

A doctor came in and announced the boy out of danger. Tom clapped his hands together and said, "I knew we'd make it!" No one said anything to him. He said what needed to be said in that statement.

He visited his grandson in the hospital every day, brought him gifts, and sneaked in ice cream. His sixty-eighth birthday arrived and left without a thought. On the day after his birthday, when he visited his grandson, the family surprised him with a cake, balloons and gifts. His grandson's card was a handwritten note thanking him for still being there. He had survived that fateful day because of his love for his grandson.

He has now broken the seventy-year mark and has come to the conclusion that he wanted to control his life. He sees that it was love for his grandson that kept him going. "Life is for living," he says now. "Death will just have to take care of itself."[59]

Application: Will we be living God's word when death comes?

Christ the King

Luke 23:35–43

The King

Theme: Though crucified, Jesus is still the King of all humankind.

During a cruel and bloody war, a commander took an oath in the presence of his troops that he would slaughter the entire population of a certain town, and in due course the bloodhounds of war were let loose on the defenseless people.

Now it so happens that a fugitive, seeking shelter, saw a sight which was indirectly the means of saving both his own life and the lives of others. He spied a number of soldiers as they broke into a house, the inmates of which they put to the sword. On leaving it, they fastened up the place again, and one of them, dipping a cloth in a pool of blood, splashed it on the door as a token to any who might follow of what had taken place inside.

Quick as his feet could carry him, the poor fugitive sped away to a large house in the center of the town where a number of his friends were concealed, and breathlessly told them what he had seen. At once it flashed upon them how to act. A goat was in the yard. It was immediately killed, and its blood splashed on the door. Scarcely could they close the door again when a band of soldiers rushed into the street and began to slay right and left. But when they came to the blood-marked door, they made no attempt to enter.

The sword—so they thought—had already entered and performed its work in that house. Thus, while the many around were put to death, all inside the blood-sprinkled door were saved.[60]

Application: Do we find joy in serving a crucified Lord and king?

Sources

Celebration
William J. Freburger, ed.
National Catholic Reporter
P.O. Box 419493
Kansas City MO 64141-6493

Connections
(newsletter of ideas, resources and
information for homilists and preachers)
Jay Cormier, ed.
Published by MediaWorks
7 Lantern Lane
Londonderry NH 03053-3905

Dynamic Preaching
King Duncan, ed.
Seven Worlds Corporation
P.O. Box 11565
Knoxville TN 37939

Five-Minute Homilies on the Gospels of Years A,B,C, 1977
Rt. Rev. Msgr. Arthur J. Tonne
Multi-Business Press
Hillsboro KS 67063

The Good News
Rev. Joseph Nolan, ed.
Liturgical Publications, Inc.
2875 South James Dr.
New Berlin WI 53151

Homily Helps
St. Anthony Messenger Press
1615 Republic St.
Cincinnati OH 45210

Homily Hints
Capsulized Communications, Ltd.
Box 968
Vernon, B.C. Canada V1T 6N2

Homily Service
Virginia Sloyan, ed.
Liturgical Conference, Inc.
8750 Georgia Ave., Suite 123
Silver Spring MD 20910-3621

Illustrated Sunday Homilies, 1987, 1988, 1989
Mark Link, S.J.
Tabor Publishing
Allen TX 75002

LectionAid
Glendon E. Harris, Publ.
P.O. Box 6300
Kamuela HI 96743-6300

Lectionary Homiletics
Lectionary Homiletics, Inc.
13540 East Boundary Rd., Building 2, Suite 105
Midlothian VA 23112

Markings
Thomas More Association
205 West Monroe St., 6th Floor
Chicago IL 60606-5097

Pastoral Life
Paulist Press
P. O. Box 595
Canfield OH 44406-0595

The Pastor's Professional Research Service
King Duncan, ed.
Seven Worlds Corporation
P.O. Box 11565
Knoxville TN 37939

Preaching the Lectionary
Reginald H. Fuller
The Liturgical Press
Collegeville MN 56321

The Priest
Our Sunday Visitor Publishing
200 Noll Plaza
Huntington IN 46750

Pulpit Digest
David Farmer, ed.
Pulpit Digest, Inc.
Logos Productions Inc.
P.O. Box 240
South St. Paul MN 55075-0240

Pulpit Resource
Glendon E. Harris, ed.
Logos Productions, Inc.
P.O. Box 240
South St. Paul MN 55075

Quotes and Anecdotes for Preachers and Teachers
Anthony P. Castle, ed.
Kevin Mayhew, Ltd.
55 Leigh Rd., Leigh-on-the Sea
Essex, England

Still Proclaiming Your Wonders, 1984
Walter J. Burghardt, S.J.
Paulist Press
997 MacArthur Blvd.
Mahwah NJ 07430

Notes
Year A

1. Brian Kelly Bauknight, *Lectionary Homiletics* (3):35, "Sermon," Nov. 1992.

2. *Homily Hints,* "Messenger of God," Sermon outline 1139, 3rd Sunday of Advent, Year A, Issue 560, Dec. 13, 1992.

3. "The Excitement of Arrival," in *Pulpit Resource* (20):41, 4th Sunday of Advent, Year A, Oct., Nov., Dec. 1992.

4. Dr. William P. Barker, *Tarbell's Teacher's Guide* (Elgin IL: David C. Cook Publishing Co., 1988) as quoted in "Victory Over Darkness," in *Dynamic Preaching* (9):23, Christmas, Dec. 1994.

5. Mike Mason, *The Mystery of the Word* (San Francisco: Harper & Row, 1988), pp. 77-84, as quoted in "Way Down in Egypt's Land," in *Dynamic Preaching* (7):26, Dec. 1992.

6. Excerpted in *Parade* Magazine, Aug. 27, 1995, as quoted in *Connections,* Holy Family Sunday, Year A, Dec. 1995.

7. "Bus 93," in *Pulpit Resource* (21):3, Jan., Feb., Mar., 1993.

8. Alex Haley, *Roots* (New York: Doubleday, 1976).

9. Charlie Appleton, "Ardmore Suspect Had Bad, Bad Day," *Nashville Banner* Aug. 30, 1990, Section A, p. 1, as quoted in "Face to Face with the Tempter," *Dynamic Preaching* (6):15, Feb. 17, 1991.

10. "Improving with Age," in *Pulpit Resource* (21):36, Jan., Feb., Mar. 1993.

11. Reprinted by permission, from "Out of Darkness," in *Pulpit Resource* (21):41, Jan., Feb., Mar. 1993. Copyright 1993 by Logos Productions, Inc.

12. Rev. Timothy Smith, "Sorry, the Doctor's Been Delayed," in *Dynamic Preaching* (8):23, Mar. 1993.

13. Jo Hart, "The Thief," from *Snowflakes in September* (Nashville: Dimensions for Living, 1992), pp. 13, 14, as quoted by Rev. Timothy Smith in "Beneath the Cross," *Dynamic Preaching* (8):5, Passion (Palm) Sunday, Apr. 1993.

14. From Louis Charbonneau-Lossey, *The Bestiary of Christ,* as quoted in *Connections,* "Psyche," Easter, Year A, Apr. 1993.

15. "Applied Science," in *Pulpit Resource* (21):10, Apr., May, June 1993.

16. "The Altar and the Marketplace," in *Connections,* 3rd Sunday of Easter, Year A, Apr. 25, 1993.

17. Pat Livingston, *Lessons of the Heart* (Notre Dame, IN: Ave Maria Press), as quoted in Rev. Pat McCloskey, O.F.M., *Homily Helps*, 4th Sunday of Easter, May 2, 1993, Series A readings, Lectionary #50, May 1993.

18. "A Church of Beggars and Princes," in *Connections*, 5th Sunday of Easter, Year A, May 1993.

19. Dorothy Pryse, *The Upper Room*. Sept./Oct. 1992, p. 23, as quoted by Rev. Timothy Smith, in "Crossing the Desert or Protecting Our Vehicle," *Dynamic Preaching* (8):26, 27, May 1993.

20. Contributed by Bruce Edwards. Source: *Confident Living*, Feb. 1993, pp. 28-29. Reprinted by permission of Back to the Bible, Inc. All rights reserved.

21. Rev. James Gilhooley, *Pastoral Life* (42):58, Pentecost, Year A, May 1993.

22. Source unknown.

23. *The Boston Globe*, Mar. 3, 1989, as quoted in "Fish Sticky,"*Connections*, Corpus Christi Sunday, Year A, May 1989.

24. "On Purpose," in *Pulpit Resource* (21):10, Jan., Feb., Mar. 1993.

25. *Canada Lutheran*, as quoted in "All One Body We," in *Pulpit Resource* (21):13, Jan., Feb., Mar. 1993.

26. Mark Link, S.J., "Pope and Prisoners," in *Illustrated Sunday Homilies* (Allen TX: Tabor Publishing), Year A, Series I, p. 53, 1987.

27. William F. Merton, "Our Argument . . . Argument too," reprinted with permission from the Oct. 1983 *Reader's Digest*, © 1983 by the Reader's Digest Assn., Inc.

28. "Room at the Inn," in *Connections*, 7th Sunday in Ordinary Time (OT), Year A, Feb. 1993.

29. "Preaching Today," as quoted in *Dynamic Preaching* (4):7, "An Invitation from the King," 4th Sunday OT, Year A, May 1989.

30. Dr. Donald Strobe, as quoted in *Dynamic Preaching* (4):28, "Extraordinary Faith," 9th Sunday OT, Year A, May 1989.

31. Ken Abraham, *Designer Genes* (Old Tappan NJ: Fleming H. Revell Company, 1986), as quoted in *Dynamic Preaching* (4):13, "The Secret of His Success," 10th Sunday OT, Year A, May 1989.

32. *Quotes and Anecdotes for Preachers and Teachers*, "Humor," p. 46, 11th Sunday OT, Year A.

33. James W. Moore, *Is There Life After Stress?* (Nashville: Dimensions for Living, 1992), p. 88, as quoted by Rev. Timothy Smith, "Confused But

Not Forgotten," in *Dynamic Preaching* (8):19, June 1993.

34. Stephen M. Crotts, "Wanted: Dead or Alive!" in *Lectionary Homiletics* (4):39-40, 13th Sunday OT, Year A, June 1993.

35. "True Freedom," in *Dynamic Preaching* (8):17, 14th Sunday OT, Year A, July 4, 1993.

36. "On and On—Stewardship Tie-In," in *LectionAid* (1):8, 15th Sunday OT, Year A, July 1993.

37. "Say the Secret Word . . . !" in *Connections*, 16th Sunday OT, Year A, July 1993.

38. Ron DelBene, *From the Heart* (Nashville: Upper Room Books, 1991), pp. 36-39. Used by permission. Quoted in "The Greatest Discovery of All," *Dynamic Preaching* (8):41, July 1993.

39. Msgr. Arthur Tonne, in *Five-Minute Homilies on the Gospels of Years A,B,C*, p. 40.

40. Source unknown.

41. From *Plough* magazine, cited in *Salt*, as quoted in "Sister of Mercy," *Connections*, 20th Sunday OT, Year A, Aug. 1993.

42. "Rest from Unrest," in *Pulpit Resource* (18):32, 21st Sunday OT, Year A, July, Aug., Sept. 1990.

43. Barbara Reynolds, "Can We Learn the Mystery of Crossing Over to Love?" *USA Today*, 13A, Feb. 26, 1993, as quoted in "Generic Christians or Disciples?" *Dynamic Preaching* (8):31, Aug. 1993.

44. "Communication," in *The Pastor's Professional Research Service*, 23rd Sunday OT, Year A, Jan., Feb. 1991.

45. "Communication," in *The Pastor's Professional Research Service*, RS 10/89-12/89 Communication 2, 23rd Sunday OT, Year A.

46. Rev. Timothy Smith, "To Forgive Is Divine," in *Dynamic Preaching* (8):25, Sept. 1993.

47. "Work," in *Quotes and Anecdotes for Preachers and Teachers*, 85, A28, 25th Sunday OT, Year A.

48. "When Actions Speak Louder Than Words," in *Dynamic Preaching* (8):35, Sept. 1993.

49. "Rebellion in the Vineyard," in *Dynamic Preaching* (8):5, 27th Sunday OT, Year A, Oct. 1993.

50. *Soundings*, as quoted in "Are You Dressed for the Banquet?" *Dynamic Preaching* (8):11, Oct. 1993.

51. "The Money Trap," in *LectionAid* (1):10, 29th Sunday OT, Year A, Oct. 1993.

52. "Jesus and the Ayatollah," in *Dynamic Preaching* (5):25, 30th Sunday OT, Year A, Oct. 1990.

53. William Barclay, as quoted by James Gilhooley, *Pastoral Life* (43):57, 31st Sunday OT, Year A, Oct. 1993.

54. Joni McCreith (North Hollywood CA) reprinted with permission from *Reader's Digest*, Sept. 1980, p. 88. © 1980 by the Reader's Digest Assn., Inc.

55. Rev. Mark Boyer, "34th Sunday OT," in *The Priest* (49):24, Year A, Nov. 1993.

56. William C. Duckworth in *Alive Now!*, 1984, p. 29, as quoted in "Relating the Text," *Pulpit Resource* (21):34, Feast of Christ the King, Year A.

57. William H. Willimon, ed., "Relating the Text," in *Pulpit Resources* (21):34, Feast of Christ the King, Year A, Nov. 1993.

Year B

1. James Gilhooley, *Pastoral Life* (41):58, Nov. 1993.

2. "The Cemetery Club," in *Connections*, Nov. 28, 1993.

3. "A Carol for the Spiritless," in *LectionAid* (1):43, Oct., Nov., Dec., 1993.

4. "Receive," in *Pulpit Resource* (18):42, 4th Sunday of Advent, Oct., Nov., Dec. 1990.

5. Tom Wilson cartoon.

6. Msgr. Arthur Tonne, "Holy Family—Your Home Is Sacred," in *Five-Minute Homilies on the Gospels of Years A,B,C*, p. 65, 1977.

7. "How Can You Tell a Christian?" in *Dynamic Preaching* (10):15, (Mother's Day) May 14, 1995.

8. Source unknown.

9. Source unknown.

10. "Rise Above It!" in *Dynamic Preaching* (6):15, 1st Sunday of Lent, Year B, Mar. 1991.

11. "Hints of the Heavenly," in *LectionAid* (1):27, Year B, Transfiguration Sunday, Feb. 13, 1994.

12. Billy Martin, autobiography *Number One*, as quoted in "I'm Mad and I'm Not Going to Take It Any More!" *Dynamic Preaching* (6):3, Mar. 1991.

13. Source unknown.

14. Source unknown.

15. Source unknown.

16. Source unknown.

17. "Rise Above It," in *Dynamic Preaching* (6):16, 5th Sunday in Lent, Mar. 1991.

18. *Quotes and Anecdotes for Preachers and Teachers*, "Word Pictures," p. 271, Passion (Palm) Sunday, Year A.

19. "A Story Almost Too Big to Tell," in *Dynamic Preaching* (6):43, Mar. 1991.

20. "A Story Almost Too Big to Tell," in *Dynamic Preaching* (6):42, Mar. 1991.

21. "Rise Above It," in *Dynamic Preaching* (6):39, Mar. 1991.

22. Philip Yancey, *Benedict Arnold Seagull*, as quoted in "Uplifting One Another," *Connections*, 2nd Sunday of Easter, Apr. 10, 1994.

23. Reprinted from *Thank God, It's Monday!* by William E. Diehl, © 1982 Fortress Press. Used by permission of Augsburg Fortress, 426 So. Fifth St., Box 1209, Minneapolis MN 55440.

24. Source unknown.

25. Msgr. Arthur Tonne, "Turn on the Light," in *Five-Minute Homilies on the Gospels of Years A,B,C*, 86.

26. "Here Comes the Bride, Rustling in White," in *Connections*, 6th Sunday of Easter, May 5, 1991.

27. "Future Testimony," in *Pulpit Resource* (19): 20, Apr., May, June 1991.

28. Source unknown.

29. "A Most Confusing Doctrine," in *Dynamic Preaching* (6):21, Trinity Sunday, May 1991.

30. Rev. Msgr. Frank Campbell, in *The Priest* (50):22, 5th Sunday OT, Jan. 1994.

31. Source unknown.

32. Calvin and Hobbes cartoon by Bill Watterson.

33. Rev. Msgr. Frank Campbell, *The Priest* (50):26, 4th Sunday OT, Jan. 1994.

34. Source unknown.

35. Anthony P. Castle, ed., *Quotes and Anecdotes for Preachers and Teachers*, p. 180, first published in Great Britain in 1979 by Kevin Mayhew, Ltd., 55 Leigh Rd., Leigh-on-the Sea, Essex.

36. Source unknown.

37. Source unknown.

38. Source unknown.

39. David Redding, *The Golden String* (Grand Rapids MI: Fleming H. Revell Co., 1988), as quoted in *Dynamic Preaching* (6):5, July 1991.

40. Mark Link, S.J., "The Seed So Small But So Powerful," in *Illustrated Sunday Homilies*, p. 73, Series I, Year B, 1988.

41. "He's Henry—I'm Donald," in *Connections*, 12th Sunday OT, June 23, 1991.

42. John Killinger, "There Is Still God," *The Twentieth Century Pulpit*, James Cox, ed. (Nashville: Abingdon Press, 1978), pp. 112-113.

43. Mark Link, S.J., "Pepe LePew," in *Illustrated Sunday Homilies*, p. 79, 1988.

44. "God's Plan for His World," in *Dynamic Preaching* (6):9, July 1991.

45. Judson Swihart, *How Do I Say I Love You?* (Downers Grove IL: Inter-Varsity Press, 1977), pp. 46-47, as quoted in "Breaking Down the Walls," *Dynamic Preaching* (6):18, July 1991.

46. "Lord, What a Bountiful God!" in *Dynamic Preaching* (6):25, July 1991.

47. Msgr. Arthur Tonne, "Thanks for the Food," in *Five-Minute Homilies on the Gospels of Years A,B,C*, p. 97, 17th Sunday OT, 1977.

48. Anthony P. Castle, ed., "Bread from Heaven," in *Quotes and Anecdotes for Preachers and Teachers*, p. 215.

49. Source unknown.

50. Source unknown.

51. "Practicing vs. Believing," in *Connections*, 22nd Sunday OT, Sept. 1991.

52. Robert S. Busey, "The Day After the Miracle," in *Lectionary Homiletics* (2):15, Sept. 1991.

53. *Salt*, Sept. 1989, as quoted in "Part and Partial," *Pulpit Resource* (19):38, Sept. 1991.

54. Msgr. Arthur Tonne, "Servant of All," in *Five-Minute Homilies on the Gospels of Years A,B,C*, p. 105, 25th Sunday OT.

55. Rev. Benedict Auer, O.S.B., "Would That All the People of the Lord Were Prophets," in *Pastoral Life* (40): 58, Sept. 1991.

56. "Cast Your Bread," in *Connections*, 27th Sunday OT, Year B, Oct. 1991.

57. Robert H. Schuller, *Success Is Never-Ending—Failure Is Never Final* (Nashville: Thomas Nelson Pub., 1988), as quoted in "The Deal of a Lifetime," *Dynamic Preaching* (6):14, Oct. 1991.

58. Alvin C. Porteous, "On Being a Man," in *Lectionary Homiletics* (2):26, Sermon from 1979, Oct. 1991.

59. Leo Rosten, *Leo Rosten's Giant Book of Laughter* (New York: Crown Pub.), p. 98.

60. *The Pastor's Professional Research Service*, Love, Nov./Dec 1990.

61. Source unknown.

62. Msgr. Arthur Tonne, "With Power and Glory," in *Five-Minute Homilies on the Gospels of Years A,B,C*, 1977, p. 114.

63. James Gilhooley, *Pastoral Life* (42): 55, Oct. 1991.

Year C

1. "Gettin' Ready for Quittin' Time," in *Dynamic Preaching* (6):6, Dec. 1991.

2. Source unknown.

3. Mark Link, S.J., "Street Preacher," in *Illustrated Sunday Homilies*, p. 7. Year C, Series I, 1989.

4. Mark Link, S.J., "Jeremiah Prophecies," in *Illustrated Sunday Homilies*, p. 7, Dec. 18, 1988.

5. Msgr. Arthur Tonne, "What Is God Like?" in *Five Minute Homilies on the Gospels of Years A,B,C*, p. 25, 5th Sunday of Easter, Year C.

6. Alvin C. Porteous, *Preaching to Suburban Captives* (Valley Forge PA: Judson Press, 1979), pp. 119-120, in *Lectionary Homiletics* (4):34, Dec. 1992. Reprinted with permission.

7. *Connections*, "Family Grace," Feast of the Holy Family, Dec. 1991.

8. *Vital Speeches*, as quoted in "Three Deadly Words," *Dynamic Preaching* (7):5, Feb. 1992.

9. Q. Wesley Allen, Jr., "A Sermon from Jan. 1989," in *Lectionary Homiletics* (3):17, Jan. 1992.

10. "Tattoos and Trauma," *Connections*, The Baptism of the Lord, Jan. 13, 1991. Quoted from *Parade* June 12, 1988, Intelligence section, Lloyd Shearer, ed.

11. Source unknown.

12. "Written Guarantee," in *Pulpit Resource* (19):29, 2nd Sunday of Lent, Feb. 24, 1991.

13. Source unknown.

14. Norm Lawson, in "Forgiveness," in *The Pastor's Professional Research Service*, PRS 3-88-1.

15. "So Who's OK?" in *Connections*, 5th Sunday of Lent, Apr. 1992.

16. Anthony P. Castle, ed., "The Suffering Servant," in *Quotes and Anecdotes for Preachers and Teachers*, p. 246, sec. B38.

17. James Gilhooley, "The Easter Vigil," in *Pastoral Life* (41):54, Year C, Apr. 18, 1992.

18. Norm Lawson, "Faith," in *The Pastor's Professional Research Service*, RS 7, 89-8/89-1.

19. Dr. Eric Ritz, "Do You Have a Forgiving Spirit?" in *Dynamic Preaching* (7):40, 3rd Sunday of Easter, Apr. 1992, p. 40. *Connections*, 4th Sunday of Easter, May 1992.

20. "The Parable of the Oboe," in *Connections*, 4th Sunday of Easter, May 1992.

21. Mark Link, S.J., "Love Story," in *Illustrated Sunday Homilies*, p. 37, Year C, Series I, 1989.

22. Source unknown.

23. "Jesus Prays for Us," in *Dynamic Preaching* (7):33, 7th Sunday of Easter, May 31, 1992.

24. *Good News* (19):663, A homily model for June 7, 1992, Pentecost, Year C.

25. Msgr. Arthur A. Tonne, "Holy Trinity—The Sun Gives Life," in *Five-Minute Homilies on the Gospels of Years A,B,C*, p. 146.

26. Source unknown.

27. Doonesbury by Gary Trudeau, Nov. 10, 1991, as quoted in *Connections*, "Today on Geraldo: Happily Married People!" 2nd Sunday OT, Jan. 1992.

28. "Ace of the Angels," by Hank Hersch. Reprinted courtesy of *Sports Illustrated*, Sept. 9, 1991. © 1991, Time, Inc. All rights reserved.

29. "Going by the Book," in *Pulpit Resource* (17):15, 4th Sunday OT, Year C, Jan., Feb., Mar. 1989.

30. Michael Heher, "Amazed and Amazing Grace," in *Markings* 1, 5th Sunday OT, Feb. 1991.

31. Walter J. Burghardt, S.J., *Still Proclaiming Your Wonders* (Ramsey NJ: Paulist Press, 1984), p. 111, 6th Sunday OT, Year C.

32. Source unknown.

33. Source unknown.

34. Anthony P. Castle, ed., in *Quotes and Anecdotes for Preachers and Teachers*, pp. 367-368.

35. *Homily Hints,* sermon outline 1257, Issue 619, 7th Sunday OT, Year C, Feb. 1995.

36. Source unknown.

37. Anthony P. Castle, ed., in *Quotes and Anecdotes for Preachers and Teachers,* p. 326.

38. Judy L. Nichols, in *Homily Helps,* 13th Sunday OT, Series C readings, Lectionary #100, June 28, 1992.

39. "Spreading the Peace," in *Homily Hints,* 14th Sunday OT, sermon outline 954.

40. Peggy Ryan, in *Markings,* homiletic reflections for July 9, 1989, 14th Sunday OT, Year C.

41. Eric Ritz, "Living Smart," in *Dynamic Preaching* (4):19, July 1989.

42. John L'Heureux, S.J., "The Trouble with Epiphanies."

43. Source unknown.

44. Benedict Auer, O.S.B., in *Pastoral Life* (41):46, 17th Sunday OT, Aug. 1992.

45. Rev. Hilarion Kistner, O.F.M., ed., in *Homily Helps,* 19th Sunday OT, Aug. 9, 1992.

46. "The Mayflower Compact?" in *Connections,* 20th Sunday OT, August 16, 1992.

47. "This Is the Moment," in *Pulpit Resource* (17):31, 21st Sunday OT, July, Aug., Sept. 1989.

48. "Friendly Love," in *Pulpit Resource* (17):36, 22nd Sunday OT, July, Aug., Sept. 1989.

49. "Concept vs Implementation," in *Connections,* Sept. 6, 1992.

50. "Peanuts" cartoon by Charles Schulz.

51. *Good News* (19):785, 25th Sunday OT, Year C, Sept. 1992.

52. Source unknown.

53. Anthony P. Castle, ed., "Go Tell Everyone," in *Quotes and Anecdotes for Preachers and Teachers,* p. 207, 27th Sunday OT, Year C.

54. "Applause, Please," in *Pulpit Resource* (17):11, Oct., Nov., Dec. 1989.

55. Source unknown.

56. Rev. Hilarion Kistner, O.F.M., ed., in *Homily Helps,* Year C, Lectionary #151, Oct. 25, 1992.

57. "Cash Flow," in *Pulpit Resource* (17):21, Oct., Nov., Dec. 1989.

58. Rev. Barbara Lundblad, "The Name of Jesus," preached on The

Protestant Hour (radio), Lutheran series, quoted in "Devising Good," *LectionAid* (17):24: Oct., Nov., Dec. 1989.

59. Dominic J. Grassi, "The Future Starts Here," in *Markings,* 33rd Sunday OT, Nov. 19, 1989.

60. Anthony P. Castle, ed., "Christ, the Covenant of God," in *Quotes and Anecdotes for Preachers and Teachers,* sec. B4, p. 152.

Of Related Interest...

Storytelling the Word
Homilies and How to Write Them
William J. Bausch

Today's parishioners are part of a visual culture, raised in a society flooded with television images. For an effective homily nowadays, listeners need word pictures. A noted homilist himself, Fr. Bausch shows how it's done in this unique book on story preaching by bringing together his years of preaching experience and extensive storytelling research.

304 pp, $14.95 (order M-64)

Telling Stories, Compelling Stories
William J. Bausch

Fr. Bausch captures the essence of the lectionary readings and makes them relevant to the Christian assembly today. The author has a wonderful ability to touch heart and head with stories that move the reader to action.

200 pages, $9.95 (order C-44)

More Telling Stories, Compelling Stories
William J. Bausch

Wonderful stories that illuminate the gospels with examples of people living as Christian role-models. These people translate grace into flesh and blood and witness to the effects of being touched and transformed by God.

200 pp, $9.95 (order C-92)

Timely Homilies
The Wit and Wisdom of an Ordinary Pastor
William J. Bausch

With warmth, insight, and vitality, Bausch demonstrates his driving commitment to helping people live God's Word. These moving homilies are rich in stories and experiences.

176 pp, $9.95 (order C-27)

Available at religious bookstores or from:

TWENTY-THIRD PUBLICATIONS

P.O. BOX 180 • 185 WILLOW ST. • MYSTIC, CT 06355 • 1-860-536-2611 • 1-800-321-0411 • FAX 1-800-572-0788

Call for a free catalog